W9-BLE-429

NEW ORLEANS

|CONDENSED|

 china williams

LONELY PLANET PUBLICATIONS
Melbourne • Oakland • London • Paris

contents

New Orleans Condensed
1st edition – March 2003

Published by
Lonely Planet Publications Pty Ltd
ABN 36 005 607 983
90 Maribyrnong St, Footscray, Vic 3011, Australia
e www.lonelyplanet.com or AOL keyword: lp

Lonely Planet offices
Australia Locked Bag 1, Footscray, Vic 3011
 ☎ 03 8379 8000 fax 03 8379 8111
 e talk2us@lonelyplanet.com.au
USA 150 Linden St, Oakland, CA 94607
 ☎ 510 893 8555 Toll Free 800 275 8555
 fax 510 893 8572
 e info@lonelyplanet.com
UK 10a Spring Place, London NW5 3BH
 ☎ 020 7428 4800 fax 020 7428 4828
 e go@lonelyplanet.co.uk
France 1 rue du Dahomey, 75011 Paris
 ☎ 01 55 25 33 00 fax 01 55 25 33 01
 e bip@lonelyplanet.fr
 www.lonelyplanet.fr

Designer Nick Stebbing Editors Danielle North &
Simon Sellars Proofer Elizabeth Swan Cartographers
Graham Neale, Laurie Mikkelsen & Sarah Sloane
Cover Designer Gerilyn Attebery Project Manager
Charles Rawlings-Way Commissioning Editor
Michele Posner Series Designer Gerilyn Attebery
Series Publishing Managers Katrina Browning &
Diana Saad Thanks to Kerryn Burgess, Darren
O'Connell, Bruce Evans, LPI & Rowan McKinnon

Photographs
All uncredited photos by Ray Laskowitz. Other images
as indicated.

Many of the photographs in this guide are available
for licensing from Lonely Planet Images:
e www.lonelyplanetimages.com
Images also used with kind permission of The New
Orleans African American Museum of Art, Culture
and History.

Front cover photographs
Top A lime green antique store on Magazine St in
the Garden District (Richard Cummins)
Bottom Silhouette of five players in a jazz band
(Marcus Amon, Stone/Getty Images)

ISBN 1 74059 455 X

Text & maps © Lonely Planet Publications Pty Ltd 2003
Photos © photographers as indicated 2003
Printed through Colorcraft Ltd, Hong Kong
Printed in China

New Orleans is the place to chill out

how to use this book

SYMBOLS

- ✉ address
- ☎ telephone number
- nearest streetcar route
- nearest bus route
- auto route, parking details
- nearest water transport
- opening hours
- tourist information
- cost, entry charge
- email/website address
- wheelchair access
- child-friendly
- on-site or nearby eatery
- good vegetarian selection

COLOR-CODING

Each chapter has a different color code which is reflected on the maps for quick reference (eg all Highlights are bright yellow on the maps).

MAPS

The fold-out maps inside the front and back covers are numbered from 1 to 6. All sights and venues in the text have map references which indicate where to find them on the maps; eg (6, J5) means Map 6, grid reference J5. Although each item is not pin-pointed on the maps, the street address is always indicated.

PRICES

Price gradings (eg $10/5) usually indicate adult/concession entry charges to a venue. Concession prices can include senior, student, member or coupon discounts.

AUTHOR AUTHOR!

China Williams

China has finally found her long-lost city – New Orleans. A place where she can talk to perfect strangers and minor celebrities, and they're all glad she took the time out for them. Other places she's test-driven have included South Carolina, Maryland, Washington, DC, Thailand and San Francisco. China now lives in Maine with her husband, Matt.

China Williams also contributed to Lonely Planet's *Georgia & the Carolinas* and *Thailand* guides.

Thanks to the entire Strachan clan (including Johanna, their adopted daughter), Sara Roahen, George Schmidt, the staff at A Creole House, my hubby and all the other sweet New Orleans folks who adopted me for a spell.

READER FEEDBACK

Things change – prices go up, schedules change, good places go bad and bad places improve or go bankrupt. So, if you find things better or worse, recently opened or long since closed, please tell us and help make the next edition even more accurate. Send all correspondence to the Lonely Planet office closest to you (listed on page 2) or visit e www.lonelyplanet.com/feedback.

Lonely Planet books provide independent advice. Lonely Planet does not accept advertising in guidebooks, nor payment in exchange for listing or endorsing any place or business. Lonely Planet writers do not accept discounts or payments in exchange for positive coverage of any sort.

facts about new orleans

At the crook of a powerful river, surrounded by swamps, New Orleans is an island, if you twist the map the right way. In her isolation she follows her own code: honor tradition and live well. Simple and seductive tenets still evident today in the effusive parades and festivals, the brass bands of young boys, the debutante parties of Uptown society. Old ways don't die out here, they are worshipped like the parade of Catholic saints or voodoo charms and potions. The populous looks backwards, not out of sentimentality, but as a reflection. The present is only an inherited image of the past.

Occupying a sinking swamp where the heat chips away at paint and paper and other evidence of human endeavors, New Orleans is unconcerned with tomorrow. The mood is about halfway through the second martini: relaxed and untroubled. The third drink toasts the city's festival season from Mardi Gras to Jazz Fest.

You'll come with great expectations: perhaps no other place looms so large in the traveler's bragging baggage as New Orleans. You'll find that the French Quarter reeks with the stench of permissiveness, the antebellum white-black lines are implicitly obeyed, and nothing really gets done, especially according to an East Coast watch. But without realizing it, you've slipped into the rhythm. Look, you've ordered a drink at breakfast. Now you're saying hello to perfect strangers on the street. Locals call it the swamp thing, an imperceptible force that erodes even the most stalwart case. You won't notice it until you return home and feel a slight tug as if you belong elsewhere, in a place where you can get your beer to go and where the heat hangs in the air like an unspoken secret; it may be two weeks or 20 years, but you'll be back, maybe for good.

Anne Rice House – beware of vampires

HISTORY

In the Beginning

Records from the 18th century document small tribes of Native Americans, collectively known as Muskogeans, living along the banks of Lake Pontchartrain and the Mississippi River. Their language was Choctaw. In other parts of the state, Houma and Choctaw tribes flourished until disease and wars with Europeans effectively destroyed the tribes and ended their traditional way of life. Intermixing did occur, especially in the early frontier days. Alliances between escaped slaves and Native Americans were common.

Sailing into Trouble

Several European explorers, among them Hernando de Soto, glimpsed the gaping mouth of the Mississippi leading into the heart of the North American continent. In 1682 René Robert Cavelier La Salle traced the Mississippi from its northern beginnings to the Gulf of Mexico, claiming everything he saw for the French king Louis XIV. For quite some time nobody really noticed or cared that La Salle named the boot-shaped wilderness at the river's end 'Louisiana.' Close to 20 years later, Pierre Le Moyne (Sieur d'Iberville) and his brother Jean-Baptiste Le Moyne (Sieur de

Bienville) entered the Mississippi and founded a colony named Nouvelle Orleans. Architect Adrien de Pauger outlined a simple grid plan in 1722 for the new city; the French Quarter still maintains his original design. Promoting the inhospitable terrain fell to John Law who convinced naive Germans, French and Swiss to join the crew of ex-convicts. Another load of prisoners and prostitutes were shipped over for good measure, and four years into the endeavor the population reached 8000.

Richard Cummins

The meandering Mississippi

Spanish Order

Desperately in need of cash, the French crown ceded Louisiana to Spain in exchange for an ally against Britain. Several years before the nearby British colonies would cast off imperial rule, New Orleans rioted against the deployed Spanish troops and demanded to remain French. Once order was enforced, the Spanish reign in New Orleans resulted in massive public works projects creating the city's first newspaper, police, successful sugarcane crop, streetlights and fire safety building codes. The colony also absorbed French refugees from the island of Haiti during the successful slave uprising in 1791, and exiled Acadians (later known as Cajuns) from British-controlled Nova Scotia settled the outlying bayous of southern Louisiana from 1765.

Louisiana Purchase & Battle of New Orleans

In 1800 the far-flung colony passed back into the hands of France, now ruled by Napoleon Bonaparte. The young nation of the US eyed the port city as an important component in western expansion and sent the US minister in Paris, Robert Livingston, to the emperor with an offer to buy New Orleans. Napoleon countered with an offer to sell the whole Louisiana territory for $15 million; the US accepted and in one highly controversial business transaction, it doubled its landmass and gained control of the entire Mississippi River. On November 30, 1803, the US flag replaced the Spanish flag in the center of Place d'Armes, now Jackson Square, thus beginning the American invasion. New England Protestants brought savvy, even cutthroat, determination to make money to the land of the Creoles. The new immigrants were shut out of the French Quarter and instead settled upriver in what is now the CBD and Garden District, where they built booming businesses and ostentatious homes.

Care's Concern

New Orleans is sometimes called the 'city that care forgot', a reference to the numerous plagues of the 18th and 19th centuries. Ships arriving from swampier regions imported more than commercial goods. Cholera killed 4430 people in 1832. Malaria had a steady diet of victims throughout those centuries. But the biggest epidemic was the yellow fever plague of 1853 when 8000 people died. The entire city became a hospital and the streets were clogged with funerals. At the time, people believed that miasmas from the dying body caused yellow fever. Others thought it was an overindulgence in food or liquor. To disturb the noxious air, cannons were fired, tar was burned, and when there was room to bury the bodies, lime was thrown on the earthen mounds. In 1882 a Cuban physician discovered that the *Aedes aegypti* mosquitoes transmitted the virus.

Shortly after Louisiana became a state in 1812, the US went to war with Britain. Most of the fighting was concentrated around Washington, DC, but a band of British troops also assembled in Jamaica for an invasion of the strategic port of New Orleans. General Andrew Jackson arrived in New Orleans to cobble together an army of trained bayou runners to repulse the impending attack. Jean Lafitte, a notorious slave smuggler, and his band of Baratarian pirates were wooed to the American side and supplied guns and ammunition. The Americans trounced the well-polished British troops at the Battle of New Orleans in Chalmette, four miles from New Orleans. This historical event, however, occurred two weeks after the treaty ending the war was signed.

Giddyap at Jackson Square

Civil War & Reconstruction

Louisiana was the sixth state to secede from the Union after the election of antislavery president Abraham Lincoln in 1860. Once fighting began, New Orleans fell to the Union one year later with the successful invasion by Captain David G Farragut's naval fleet. It was the first Confederate city to be occupied and would remain under military control for 15 years, longer than any other 'reconstructed' city. The federal occupation army was led by General Benjamin Butler, who was so despised by New Orleanians that 'butlerize' became synonymous with 'stealing,' referring to the practice of confiscating property if the owner didn't pledge allegiance to the Union. Even today, many old families recount finding their families' stolen silver in New England homes, generations later.

Rioting and vigilante terror groups organized to thwart the federally imposed civil liberties given to the freed slaves before and after home rule

was reestablished during the 1870s. Once the white government regained control, it passed a state act that enforced racial segregation on public vehicles and other revocations of civil liberties. Like the rest of the former slave states, Louisiana, and its cultural capital of New Orleans, struggled against modernity and its bitter loss to the North by recreating and romanticizing a master-slave hierarchy.

An influx of European immigrants, mainly Sicilian and Irish, poured into the city for economic opportunities. The Italians settled into the French Quarter, which had been abandoned by Creole families during the unrest of the Civil War or earlier for more fashionable homes uptown.

St Louis Cathedral

D'oh! Homer Arrested for Sitting on Train

Homer Adolph Plessy was one-eighth black (by law a Negro) but was so light skinned that he could pass undetected as white; in 1896 he boarded a public train, sat in the whites-only section and let the proper authorities know of his legal race. He was arrested, and *Plessy v Ferguson* filtered through the courts system to the Supreme Court where the constitutionality of Louisiana's law was upheld and an era of legalized discrimination sanctioned. This 'separate but equal' system of segregation persisted almost sixty years, until it was overturned by the landmark civil-rights case *Brown v Board of Education* in 1954.

Modern Times

Racial struggles persisted into the 20th century and beyond. Many whites moved to the suburbs after the US government dismantled the South's segregation laws. In 1978 the city elected its first black mayor, Ernest N Morial, ushering in a more integrated city government. At the turn of the 21st century, New Orleans seemed partially poised for a resurgence. Crime rates had dropped, neighborhoods were being revitalized and the new major Ray Nagin promised to clean up the city's entrenched culture of corruption.

Louis Armstrong

New Orleans' beloved cornetist Louis Armstrong grew up in the area called back o' town around Liberty and Perdido Sts. At the age of 12 he was sent to reform school where he learned to play first the bugle and then the cornet. Before his musical career took off, he unloaded banana boats and delivered coal and milk. Armstrong joined King Oliver's Creole Jazz Band in Chicago in 1922 and later embarked on a solo career in New York City. In 1931 he returned home to New Orleans as a star and was honored as king of the Zulus, a Mardi Gras krewe (a club that sponsors Mardi Gras parades and other events). Not too shabby.

ORIENTATION

Because the river runs such a meandering course and New Orleanians are unconcerned with naming conventions, the cardinal points of the compass are virtually useless here. All directions in New Orleans are given in relation to the river (roughly to the south) or Lake Pontchartrain (to the north). 'Above' and 'below' describe a location relative to the flow of the river. For example, the convention center is 'above' the French Quarter (or upriver). 'Riverside' (in the direction of the river) and 'lakeside' (in the direction of the lake) are also used in orientation. Louis Armstrong Park is on the lake side of the French Quarter. The lake might still be far away, but if you're going that direction then you're not going to the river. Got it? Once you arrive in New Orleans-land, it will all make more sense. Actually finding addresses is quite easy because the blocks are numbered by 100s from the river or from either side of Canal St. So the 400 block of St Charles Ave shares a cross-street with the 400 block of Camp St.

Gallier Hall – Greek revival at its best

ENVIRONMENT

In addition to its other big-city problems, such as air and water pollution, New Orleans has a difficult relationship with its watercourses, one of tenuous peace. The city's lack of elevation averages 2ft below sea level, and a series of levees and spillways thwart water's encroachment into this natural saucer. As late as the 1940s, dense swamplands extended from the lake to the city limits acting as natural floodwalls. Most of these swamps have now been converted into subdivisions, requiring extra pumping capacity and increasing the city's vulnerability to massive flooding, should the Mississippi jump its banks. If common wisdom of 100-year floods holds water, 2027 will be a very bad year for the Crescent City.

GOVERNMENT & POLITICS

The state of Louisiana is organized into parishes, which means geographical units defined long ago by the Catholic Church. New Orleans falls into Orleans Parish, which is governed by an elected mayor and a city council. At the time of writing, the mayor was Ray Nagin, who took office in early 2002. Unlike other US states, which base civil laws on English cases, Louisiana bases its laws on the Napoleonic Code of France.

ECONOMY

The Mississippi River has supported New Orleans since the city's birth; the invention of the steamboat in the early 19th century ushered in the port's Golden Age. New Orleans became the commercial hub for outgoing cotton, sugar and rice, and incoming coffee, fruit and luxury goods. By 1850 New Orleans was also the largest slave-trading center in the US. During this time, the population boomed, making New Orleans the third largest city in the US by 1830. Satellite industries centered on particular streets in the CBD: the cotton brokers on Carondelet St, newspapers on Poydras Ave, banks on Camp St.

In the 1960s Miami began to eclipse New Orleans as a favored trading partner with Latin America, and Houston took another bite out of New Orleans' shrinking shipping claims. Today, the port receives 4000 ships annually; these constitute about 15% of the total tonnage in US ports. Latin America is still the largest trade partner, and maritime-related jobs make up about 9% of the economy. During a recent 'state of the port' address, officials described the port's health as stable, having recovered from changing trade relations, import regulations and international conditions.

Did you know?

- New Orleans' population is approximately 500,000 people.
- A 'luxury' one bedroom condo in the French Quarter costs $1000 to $1300 per month.
- New Orleans receives 11.3 million visitors per year.
- French was the official language of Louisiana until 1921.
- In 1945 New Orleans had 108 miles of canals (Venice only 28).
- New Orleans finishes in 2nd place behind Las Vegas as a wedding and honeymoon destination.

More promising for the port is the growing cruise ship industry. Weekly sailings on major lines depart from New Orleans or stay overnight en route to Mexico and South America. On average about half a million people visit the city as part of a cruise stop per year, and that number is expected to increase as cruise companies replace smaller vessels with large ones able to carry 2000 to 3000 passengers.

Tourism, however, is the biggest employer, with a 29% share of the economy. Oddly, tourism isn't the biggest money maker; that title goes to the oil and gas industry, which goes through almost daily boom and bust periods.

SOCIETY & CULTURE

New Orleanians make laid-back living deliciously enticing. Utmost on the day's list is having a good time, which usually entails food, drink and conversation. They'll talk to anyone who'll listen and will spin fantastic yarns unapologetically cloaked as history. The city abounds with so many unselfconscious eccentrics that you might wonder if you're the oddball for noticing. Even the cloistered society types are strangely democratic and remarkably outgoing.

The drawback is that nothing much gets done and rarely are people in a rush, which can be frustrating if you're waiting for a meal or a repair on a broken air-con unit. The Creoles and the Americans clashed over industriousness more than a hundred years ago, and the languid Creole way won – maybe there is a good reason for this.

In New Orleans proper, African Americans hold a 62% majority, with whites comprising 35% and Hispanics 3% of the population. A large community of Southeast Asians, predominantly Vietnamese, live in the far eastern suburbs of the city. Although the distribution of power and wealth is unbalanced, the city enjoys a unique position in modern race relations thanks to the legacy of free people of color, a group composed of antebellum freed slaves and the children of mixed relationships. Free people of color owned property, were educated and practised skilled trades long before those inalienable rights were won for everyone.

See what can happen after a few drinks at Pat O'Briens?

Etiquette

New Orleans is very Southern in its social etiquette. Greeting people on the street and generously dispensing 'thank yous' and 'pleases' helps to put locals at ease. You'll receive in return lots of 'honeys' and 'sweeties' from the clerk taking your food order or the chambermaid returning home on the bus. These pleasantries help draw you into the Crescent City's ample bosom of family and friends.

ARTS
Architecture

If you hate good food and despise a good time, then New Orleans is still worth it for the architecture alone. In the French Quarter, chipped stuccoed buildings with their lacy ironwork balconies pose like mantilla-veiled Spanish maidens. These were built during the Spanish occupation and bear the initials of their first owners in the balconies' detailed patterns. Huddled in the residential section of the Quarter, the simple shuttered Creole townhouses are more suggestive of the Caribbean than the American South with their coral-colored facades faded by the sun. The Creole cottages are constructed flush to the sidewalk, creating an impregnable fence and daring passersby to peek through the louvered shutters. Their eaves hang over the sidewalk, sheltering people from the sun and rain. During Victorian times the austere fronts were decorated with swirling lintels and gables as if a young girl were playing dress-up with her mother's jewelry. Equally interesting for a cottage connoisseur are the brightly painted Creole cottages of the Faubourg Marigny.

The simple Creole domiciles seem like quaint garages compared to the totalitarian Greek revival mansions in the Garden District and Uptown. The

Cute Creole cottage in the Quarter

nouveau riche Americans were as competitive in their house building as they were in their businesses. Lofty columns, alabaster facades and etched glass details were all assembled to create minicastles for a people deprived of a monarchy. Along the wide canopied avenues, the branches of the noble live oaks match the arabesque of the Spanish-style cast-iron balconies imported from the French Quarter.

Music

The brash sounds of brass instruments found an eternal home in New Orleans never to be deposed as more modern trends swept the nation. The post–Civil War marching bands first introduced the populace to the powerful belch of the tuba, the blue cry of the trumpet, the heartbeat of the bass drum. Once the brass found their way into the hands of the city's African Americans, the result was jazz.

Two native sons are credited with rearing America's indigenous music. Cornetist Buddy Bolden steered ragtime into jazz time and Louis Armstrong made it swing. A group of white musicians, called the Original Dixieland Jazz Band, smuggled the New Orleans sound out of the city to the rest of the nation in 1917. Some mark them as thieves; others are more sympathetic, realizing that white ambassadors were a conduit for jazz's voyage from obscure folk music to American classical music.

Jazz went on to meet other musical sculptors in Memphis, Chicago, New York and Kansas City. In its hometown it stayed true to the horns, which presided over funerals, parades and cocktail parties. Even today lanky kids outsized by their instruments play the songs of long ago with modern inflections: a little rap, a little R&B and a whole lot of soul.

Other musicians and musical styles flourished within a local cult of celebrity with a few national exports. Professor Longhair rolled out popular good-times songs on his piano. Fats Domino crooned his way to Top 40 fame. The Neville Brothers became the first family of New Orleans R&B for many decades. As a graying man revisiting the streets of his youth, Wynton Marsalis brought the music back home with his post–Miles Davis jazz. But it's not the exports that define New Orleans' vibrant music scene; it is the small-town darlings who make a living out of moving people to dance and sing.

Leisure Listening

For a brief overview of New Orleans' musical heritage check out the following albums:

- Louis Armstrong, *Louis Armstrong 1925-1926* (Chronological Classics)
- Jelly Roll Morton, *Jelly Roll Morton 1939-1940* (Chronological Classics)
- Professor Longhair, *Collector's Choice* (Rounder, 1950s)
- Dirty Dozen Brass Band, *Voodoo* (Columbia, 1989)
- Wynton Marsalis, *Standard Time Vol 3 The Resolution of Romance* (Sony, 1990)

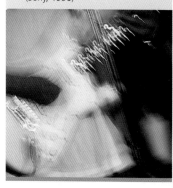

Literature

New Orleans has been a muse to many great authors. George Washington Cable (1844-1925) found rich fodder for his fictional books *Old Creole Days* and *The Grandissimes*. Most damning was his essay *The Negro Question*, which dealt with Louisiana's *Code Noir* (regulations dating from 1724 that limited the movements and rights of blacks). In *The Awakening,* Kate Chopin (1851-1904) wrote about a character who discovers the leisure class' malaise amid the Garden District's lavish homes. While living at 636 St Peter St, Tennessee Williams wrote *A Streetcar Named Desire* (1947), which he had originally set in Chicago. Walker Percy's first novel, *The Moviegoer* (1961), hauntingly taps into the despair that drives New Orleans toward incessant parties.

Fittingly, the most 'New Orleans' novel is a straightforward tale of the wacky citizens who make this city more than just a sweaty swamp. John Kennedy Toole's first novel *A Confederacy of Dunces* (1980), about an overweight hot dog vendor, so perfectly captures almost every segment of the society that his characters can still be spotted on the street today.

highlights

New Orleans' festivals, like Mardi Gras and Jazz Fest, are its biggest draws and are spectacles unto themselves, leaving the visitor little time to truly explore the city. To get to know this modern anachronism, come during the off-season, especially during the week; this is when you'll be able to get a seat at the famous restaurants, wander the streets of the French Quarter without getting stuck behind a fighting family, and ride the streetcar with the commuters. Unlike most US cities, New Orleans isn't action-packed with museums and cultural centers and the buzz of commerce. The pace is slow and if you find you've exhausted your itinerary then you're moving too fast. Fill the day with a ramble, a meal, a cocktail and lots of live music.

Lowlights of New Orleans
- Crummy French Quarter hotels that charge upscale prices
- A pitiful economy with the associated problems of poverty and crime
- The stagnation that results from eons of corruption
- No right-of-way for pedestrians
- Tourists who don't know how to politely share the sidewalk

Stopping Over

One Day Start the day with beignets and café au lait at Cafe du Monde. Stroll the French Market, Royal St and Esplanade Ave for an unstructured appreciation of the French Quarter's architecture. For lunch grab a muffuletta at Luigi's, some raw oysters at Acme or a fried oyster po'boy at Johnny's. Visit the jazz exhibit at the US Mint or the Mardi Gras exhibit at the Presbytère. Make dinner reservations at K-Paul's Louisiana Kitchen. Afterwards do some French Quarter barhopping (Napoleon House, Pat O'Brien's, Lafitte's Blacksmith Shop) and imbibe the wee hours with some Bourbon St madness.

Two Days Do an eye-opening brunch at Brennan's to shake off the hangover. For the eager beavers, a morning walking tour of the cemeteries or the history of the French Quarter will work up an appetite for an early lunch at Uglesich's. Take the St Charles streetcar uptown to the end, or get off in the Garden District for a stroll. Grab an evening cocktail at the Columns Hotel and eat dinner at one of the city's contemporary restaurants such as Bayona, Peristyle or Emeril's. Celebrate late into the night at one of the smokin' music clubs.

Three Days Take a cooking class or visit the Ogden Museum of Southern Art and the nearby Julia St galleries. Dress up for a formal, all-day meal at one of the old-line restaurants such as Galatoire's, Commander's Palace or Antoine's. Or head out for a shopping spree on Magazine St. Toast the crescent bend in the Mississippi at the 360 Bar. Do a soul food dinner at Dooky Chase or Praline Connection, which also has a Sunday gospel brunch. Cruise the hip nightclubs of Frenchmen St before catching another late-night music show.

JAZZ FEST (4, G4)

In the city credited with inventing jazz, this premier festival celebrates music, community and good times like no other. The voices and instruments that are stuffed into dark clubs most of the year get to meet the glorious summer sun and a sea of smiling faces. More than 12 stages host jazz, zydeco, R&B, bluegrass, gospel and rock. Let your ears be your guide to a lifelong hero or a new found legend.

As an accompaniment, food stalls run by local restaurants and homegrown personalities dish up some of the city's famous cuisine, from po'boys and boiled crawfish to gumbo and fried chicken. Let your nose be your guide. Local artists and craftspeople also set up shop along the perimeter.

In addition to the daytime shows, evening concerts are held all over the city throughout the festival. You can check the schedule as early as the preceding January.

The festival was launched in 1968 attracting native son Louis Armstrong and jazz legend Dave Brubeck, with minimal success. The next year it moved to the Fair Grounds and featured other music genres. Now it is so wildly popular that the good times are a little watered down with complaints of long lines and inconsiderate attendees. Jazz Fest is a big draw with over 500,000 in attendance; it requires patience and advance planning, especially when you're making hotel reservations. Prepare for tropical temperatures: drink lots of water, wear sunscreen and stand in the shade. Bring a blanket to sit on, some extra toilet paper and a rain poncho.

INFORMATION

- ✉ 1751 Gentilly Blvd
- e www.nojazzfest.com
- 🚌 shuttle from downtown $10 round trip or No 48 Esplanade bus
- 🚗 limited parking $20
- ◷ last weekend in April-1st weekend in May, 11am-7pm
- ⑤ $18 in advance or $25 at the gate
- ⓘ New Orleans Jazz & Heritage Festival (1205 N Rampart St, New Orleans, LA 70116; ☎ 522-4786); buy tickets from Ticketmaster (☎ 522-5555)
- ♿ information line ☎ 558-6140

DON'T MISS • gospel tent • crawfish bread • any local act • Jazz Fest posters

INFORMATION

ⓘ For more information, see *Arthur Hardy's Mardi Gras Guide*, available in bookstores each year before Twelfth Night. *Gambit* and *Offbeat* also publish guides to Mardi Gras. Or contact the New Orleans Metropolitan Convention and Visitors Bureau (☎ 566-5003; 800-672-6124; e www .neworleanscvb.com).

MARDI GRAS

A city-wide party devoted to imbibing incognito – what a marvelous idea. Everyone in New Orleans turns their attention to this celebration of doing it all before it's too late. Grown men dress up in elf shoes and tights like fairy-book princes. The mayor cedes power for the day to some guy calling himself Rex. Grandmas and children scrap over plastic beads thrown by people dressed up like court jesters. Music emanates from every corner and the whole city grins.

This Catholic holiday has bawdy pagan origins. Mardi Gras can be traced to the pre-spring rituals of the Romans, when class and identity were hidden behind masks, social conventions were flouted and hedonism embraced. It came to be known as *'carnevale'* (farewell to flesh), referring to the fast that would begin on Ash Wednesday.

The theatrical nature of Carnival, with its elaborate baroque costumes, was inherited from 17th-century Venice and its *commedia dell'arte*. France eventually imported the spectacle to its New World outpost of Nouvelle Orleans.

In its new home, the Creoles threw elaborate masquerade balls allowing the color lines to be crossed by the disguised attendants, especially by Creole men interested in quadroon women (women of one-quarter African blood). The Creole custom seemed to indulge the spirit of hedonism under the veil of social decorum. Large outdoor gatherings were prohibited as violence and rioting often erupted.

Future Mardi Gras Dates

Since Fat Tuesday is pegged to the lunar holiday of Easter, it can occur on any Tuesday between February 3 and March 9.

2003	March 4
2004	February 24
2005	February 8
2006	February 28
2007	February 20
2008	February 5

DON'T MISS • wearing a costume • Endymion, with the biggest float in New Orleans, parading Saturday night • Orpheus, led by Harry Connick Jr and a cast of celebrities, parading Monday night

Experiencing Carnival

The Carnival season begins on January 6 (Twelfth Night) and runs until Mardi Gras day (Fat Tuesday), which varies every year. A small St Charles Ave parade and low-key balls, some open to the public, start the season with a slow methodical rhythm. A bawdy foot parade travels through the French Quarter three Saturdays before Fat Tuesday. The real parade season starts 12 days before Fat Tuesday. On Lundi Gras (the day before Mardi Gras), the keys to the city are ceremoniously turned over by the mayor to the King of Rex. The major parade routes are the **Uptown Route** (St Charles Ave from Napoleon Ave to Canal St) and the **Mid City Route** (City Park down Orleans Ave to Carrollton Ave to Canal St). The grandstands (with paid admission) are set up in front of Gallier Hall in the CBD. Although visitors can't gain access to the society balls where the older krewes crown their kings and queens, modern krewes throw parties that are open to the public. For tickets, call Orpheus (☎ 822-7211), Tucks (☎ 288-2481) or the gay krewe Petronius (☎ 525-4498).

The modern practice of parading during Mardi Gras didn't evolve until the mid-19th century when an elite group of Americans from the Garden District (called the Mistick Krewe of Comus) publicly launched their torch-lit floats in 1857. Mimicking European royalty, the krewes crowned a king who was disguised by a beard, a beaded crown and regal garb. The king was then paraded in public on elaborate floats, often thematically decorated.

The krewe of Rex added the official colors of Mardi Gras: purple for justice, green for faith and gold for power. They named their king the 'King of Mardi Gras' and the supreme official of the city during the festival.

The now extinct Twelfth Night Revelers introduced 'throws,' which are trinkets tossed to the crowd as the floats pass by. These keepsakes are highly collectible and often depict the krewe's seal or trademark.

During this time the racially divided South did not mix during Mardi Gras. In 1885 the Mardi Gras Indians emerged from the backstreets of the African-American community. Their dress was modeled after the traditional dress of Native Americans, the 'gangs' would parade on foot in their hand-assembled, elaborately feathered head-dresses and body suits chanting inherited songs.

Unmask your true self

The most socially evocative group was the Zulus, an African-American krewe who appeared in 1909. Parodying the royal aspects of the white krewes and the popular minstrel shows of the day, the Zulus wore black faces and pseudotribal grass skirts; they crowned their king with a lard-can crown and a banana-stalk scepter. Louis Armstrong reigned as King Zulu in 1949. Today, the Zulus have one of the most prized throws: a painted coconut.

DON'T MISS
• Zulus on Mardi Gras morning parading a portion of the Uptown route • the Rex float with the *boeuf gras* (fatted cow) float on Mardi Gras morning

FRENCH QUARTER   (MAP 6)

The oldest sector of New Orleans, the French Quarter, is by far the most charming and historical. Visitors come to wander the compact streets and enjoy the architecture. Almost every home has a bricked courtyard or patio, decorated with a fountain and tropical banana trees, ginger plants or palms. The aged beauty of the Quarter truly emerges just after a thunderstorm, when streaks of gold, peach and violet reflect off the ornate cast-iron balconies where hanging ferns grow more verdant in the saturated light.

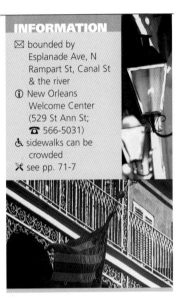

INFORMATION

✉ bounded by
  Esplanade Ave, N
  Rampart St, Canal St
  & the river
ⓘ New Orleans
  Welcome Center
  (529 St Ann St;
  ☎ 566-5031)
♿ sidewalks can be
  crowded
✗ see pp. 71-7

The Quarter (also known as the Vieux Carré or Old Square) was laid out in a gridlike pattern in 1721 by French engineers. Of the original French buildings, only the **Ursuline Convent** survived the two fires that destroyed the city. The Spanish rebuilt the city, introducing brick fire walls and ceramic tiled roofs as fireproofing measures. They also imprinted the district with its distinctive decorative ironwork.

Many of the original inhabitants were Creole plantation owners who would winter in the city. They would arrive in time for midnight mass at St Louis Cathedral on Christmas Eve and stay through the Mardi Gras season, returning to their Mississippi River plantations on Ash Wednesday.

By the early 20th century, many of the original Creole families had died out or moved to more fashionable neighborhoods. The French Quarter fell into disrepair and was scheduled to be razed before preservation efforts of the 1930s saved the district. Restoration of the old houses was so successful that very few people can afford to live in the Quarter these days, and buildings that go on the market are quickly converted into hotels for the tourist industry.

Ursuline Convent

DON'T MISS

• Jackson Square (p. 20) • Bourbon St (p. 19) • French Quarter walking tour (p. 46) • Labranche Building (p. 36) • Madam John's Legacy (p. 37)

BOURBON ST   (6, H4)

King of convenience, an entertainment 7-Eleven, a 24-7 carnival. You can get everything here – booze, strippers, music, food. You might go here out of curiosity. The day has turned to indigo dusk, the neon lights blaze with silent intensity and the steady flow of human traffic has squeezed out the cars. The bars blare rock cover tunes and a crowd has assembled around a balcony where Mardi Gras beads are being dispensed in exchange for a flash of some flesh. The wholesome-looking housewife is usually the first to take the bait, expertly lifting her top to deafening cheers. Bourbon St unloosens people at the seams. Next thing you know you've wandered into a techno-thumping, harshly lit daiquiri joint, waffling between sips of a 'triple bypass' or 'nuclear holocaust.' 'No,' you tell the pimpled teenager behind the counter, 'give me a large.' You join the crowd, swept up in the party atmosphere. You might run one end of the street to the other before venturing into one of the packed clubs where waiters hawk test tubes of fluorescent-colored liquor and sweaty bodies bump into each other.

INFORMATION

- ✉ bounded by Canal St & Esplanade Ave, btw Dauphine & Royal Sts
- ◷ 8 blocks are closed to motor vehicles after dark; bar times vary
- ♿ sidewalks can be crowded
- ✗ Clover Grill (p. 73), Verti Mart (p. 77)

You don't need a guide to Bourbon St. It is self-explanatory: go with cash and spend it on whatever you want. Have a good time. Get drunk, yell, vomit, dance, slobber on your friend, stay up till dawn. It all goes here and it goes every night, all night.

Laissez les bons temps rouler (let the good times roll).

You'll never be lonely on Bourbon St

DON'T MISS • trying at least three ridiculously named frozen drinks • buying a cheap feather boa • tipping the Michael Jackson lookalike • getting schnockered and making an ass of yourself

JACKSON SQUARE (6, G6)

With a front-row view of the Mississippi River, Jackson Square and its surrounding buildings were the city's nerve center during the colonial period. Originally named Place d'Armes, the square was rededicated to the hero of the

Battle of New Orleans, Andrew Jackson, in 1856 with a snapshot-like sculpture of the general tipping his hat in adieu, astride his rearing horse.

Facing the square, the triple-spired **St Louis Cathedral** was the spiritual focal point for the Creole populace. Dedicated to Louis IX, France's sainted king, the church was completed in 1794, with significant remodeling in 1851. The interior of the church is renaissance and baroque, with many ornate murals and side chapels.

If facing the cathedral, to your left is the **Cabildo**, the meeting house for the Spanish and French governments during their respective terms. The Louisiana Purchase was signed here. Now it houses a museum on Louisiana and New Orleans history.

The Cabildo's twin, on the other side of the cathedral, is the **Presbytère**, which served many purposes during the colonial period. It is now home to the Louisiana State Museum's Mardi Gras exhibit.

Facing each other from across the square are the block-long **Pontalba Apartments**, constructed in 1850 by Madame Michaëla Pontalba. She was the daughter of Don Andres Almonester y Roxas, the Spanish benefactor who funded the rebuilding of the Cabildo, Presbytère and cathedral after the citywide fires. Her story is more interesting than her legacy of row houses. She grew up in a wealthy and powerful New Orleans family and was joined to another prominent family through marriage. The couple moved to Paris where the husband's family attempted to procure her fortune; she resisted and eventually separated from her husband. Frustrated by this, the father-in-law shot her and then turned the gun on himself. Madame Pontalba recovered from the wounds and returned to New Orleans in 1844. She refurbished the buildings on Jackson Square, adding mansard roofs to the Cabildo and Presbytère, and building the arcaded row houses bearing her name.

The **1850 House Museum** (p. 35) has a self-guided tour through a period-decorated apartment in the Lower Pontalba building.

DON'T MISS
• free tour of St Louis Cathedral • watching the buskers and musicians performing in the square • view of Jackson Square from Moonwalk Park (p. 40)

OLD US MINT   (6, F8)

George Gershwin described jazz as an American folk music that courses through the people's veins more than any other style. Sociologically jazz is the neutral ground where whites and blacks trade their cultural heritage – a place outside of location where European instruments meet African syncopation and invention.

One of the first dialogues occurred in New Orleans where European operas and Congo Square's African dances joined the city's celebration of music. Local cornetist Buddy Bolden (1877-1931) is credited with being the 'King of Jazz.' Whether he was the first or the best is lost to history, but mythic stories recount that Bolden once played his cornet so loudly that it actually exploded. His energetic style influenced leagues of younger New Orleans musicians, including cornetist Joe 'King' Oliver (1885-1938), trombonist Kid Ory (1886-1973) and piano player Jelly Roll Morton (1890-1941). Morton, incidentally, claimed to have invented jazz in a Storyville bordello in 1902; historians believe that Morton, who was musically trained, recorded the emerging jazz sound played by musicians who couldn't read music.

INFORMATION

- ✉ 400 Esplanade Ave
- ☎ 568-6968
- e lsm.crt.state.la.us
- ⊙ Tues-Sun 9am-5pm
- $ $5/4
- ♿ good
- ✗ Old Dog New Trick Cafe (p. 76)

New Orleans' most famous musician, Louis 'Satchmo' Armstrong (1901-71), came of age during the 1920s under the tutelage of King Oliver and Kid Ory. He gave jazz a swing that was so frequently mimicked that his music seems conventional today. Other Crescent City stars include soprano saxophonist Sidney Bechet, clarinetist Barney Bigard and trumpeter Louis Prima.

The New Orleans jazz exhibit at the Old US Mint recounts this history with displays of sheet music, instruments, soundtracks and artists' biographies. The instruments that sing the notes are also featured, with a helpful musical breakdown for nonmusicians. Even lukewarm jazz enthusiasts will be intrigued by the room filled with candid shots of New Orleans musicians and jazz funerals.

Incidentally the building operated as a mint from 1838 to 1909; the small 1st-floor exhibit covers this period. Additional exhibits include Newcomb pottery and Houma Indian art.

DON'T MISS
• Louis Armstrong's childhood bugle and cornet • the handwritten note by a young Harry Connick Jr to Armand Hug • historic photos of childhood bands • the homemade drum set of street performer Cocomo Joe

FRENCH MARKET (6, F7)

A gleaming gold-leafed statue of Joan of Arc riding into battle leads the procession of shops hitched to the pavilion of stalls known as the French Market. Composed of two parts (the flea market and farmers market), the French Market earned its name from the French settlers who established a food bazaar here around 1791, but the tradition of trading on this ground can be traced back to pre-colonial days. Native Americans came here to barter sassafras leaves and hides with the early Europeans. Nowadays a spirit of bargaining persists, but the purchases vastly differ. Stall workers can suck the curious into an expert game of 'name the price' on silver bracelets, sunglasses, knockoff designer purses, Mardi Gras paraphernalia, concert posters and T-shirts.

INFORMATION
- ✉ Decatur St from St Ann St to Barracks St
- ⊘ 9am-5pm
- ⑤ free
- ♿ fair
- ✕ Cafe du Monde (p. 72)

The small farmers market sells satsumas and other local produce wearied from the day's heat; this isn't the place to come to fill a grocery list or to find fiber to offset the New Orleans fried food obsession. It is, however, the place to score some ass-kickin' hot sauces with equally obscene names. The farmers market used to be the leading greengrocer in the French Quarter, having easy access to the docked boats bearing fruits from distant climes. Stalls sprawled all along the river as far uptown as Cafe du Monde, where the German butchers convened. John James Audubon described the public market as 'the dirtiest place in America.' Now that the carcasses are gone, the filth award could easily go to Bourbon St.

DON'T MISS
- musicians who play in the nearby cafés • the public restroom near the farmers market

NEW ORLEANS CUISINE

New Orleans' cuisine is called Creole, and to describe its origins is to recount the city's history. In the beginning there was French food, characterized by rich sauces and pureed soups, constructed from a base called roux (flour browned with fat) and *mirepoix* (sauteed celery, onions and carrots). The Spanish came along and swapped bell peppers for carrots, which didn't like the Louisiana heat. Seasonings from the New World forests, such as bay leaves, cayenne pepper and filé (ground sassafras), were added by Native Americans. The miniature lobster, known as crawfish, and other fruits of the sea were also directed into the pot from Native American fishing holes. The Africans com-

INFORMATION

⊘ many restaurants outside the French Quarter are closed Sun

ⓘ restaurant reviews in *Best of New Orleans* and *Times-Picayune*

& good

manding the kitchens introduced the method of slow cooking and deep frying. Okra, an African refugee, also joined the melange as a thickening agent. These ingredients are the beginnings of New Orleans' most famous exports – jambalaya, red beans and rice, and gumbo.

With the exception of gumbo, the dishes that get touted as 'New Orleans cuisine' in the rest of the country aren't the city's true culinary stars, but rather everyday staples best enjoyed at grandma's house or from the corner deli. The real celebrities of Creole cuisine are dishes with a closer allegiance to France; these include the house interpretation of baked oysters, duck confit, sherry-spiked turtle soup or *poisson en papillote* (fish cooked in parchment paper).

The cuisine's staples speak of a boundless harvest where forests and waters provide seasonal variety. Trout, snapper, pompano, blue crab, shrimp, oysters and crawfish are handled in countless ways; they are sauteed in butter, deep-fried in cornmeal batter, or boiled with copious amounts of spices. If a little is good – goes the New Orleans' maxim – more is better. Unique to most American menus is the appearance of wild game, especially duck. Swamp dwellers, such as alligator, turtle and frogs, are also commonplace at a New Orleans table.

Creole versus Cajun

In the watery Louisiana backwoods, French exiles from Nova Scotia put a similar set of ingredients, such as seafood and game, over the fire to boil. Their cuisine (and culture) came to be called Cajun and reflected ethnic influences similar to those of Cajun's cosmopolitan cousin, Creole. Cajun cooking, however, is simpler and further removed from traditional French cuisine. Andouille gumbo and crawfish etouffee might appear at both Cajun and Creole tables; while boudin sausage and cracklins (deep-fried pork skin) are Creole comfort food.

CITY PARK (4, F3)

The proud live oaks draped in Spanish moss combined with the first-rate museum, theme parks and botanical garden make City Park a well-rounded family destination.

Founded in 1910, **New Orleans Museum of Art** (4, F3) was a gift from local philanthropist Isaac Delgado. The permanent exhibits on the 2nd floor waltz through Western art from 17th-century Dutch to 20th-century American. Edgar Degas' *Portrait of Madame René de Gas* was painted in New Orleans, just a few blocks from the museum. Art haters might be impressed by the photography exhibit; in one cool shot a young Elvis Presley steps out of a car in downtown New Orleans. A small collection of Fabergé and Louisiana work round out the 2nd-floor collection.

On the 3rd floor, there is a sizable assortment of Asian, African and pre-Columbian art and artifacts.

The **Botanical Garden** (4, F3) offers a 12-acre course on Louisiana flora. Designed and built by the federal works project, the garden features a unique Art Deco pond surrounded by bricked paths, a rose garden and a butterfly garden.

Popular children's fairytales have been translated into a playground at **Storyland** (4, F2). Children can climb aboard Peter Pan's pirate ship, slide down Jack & Jill's hill, or search for Pinocchio in the belly of the whale. It'll make you wish you were under 4ft tall.

A renovated 1906 carousel with a working Wurlitzer organ and stained-glass cupola is the centerpiece at **Carousel Gardens** (4, F2). Other rides include a small roller coaster, bumper cars and other county fair regulars.

Many swords and pistols have been drawn at somber **Dueling Oaks** (4, F3), of which only one original tree remains. One famous duel involved the master fencer Gilbert Rosiere. The opera and the theater frequently moved Gilbert to tears, and on one occasion, a man seated next to him laughed at this display. The offended Gilbert threw his glove, indicating a challenge to a duel. In the end, sensitive Gilbert spared the man's life but left him with a disfiguring scar, a reminder to laugh only at people who aren't fencers.

INFORMATION

- ⊠ Esplanade Ave & Wisner Blvd
- ☎ 482-4888
- e www.neworleanscitypark.com
- 🚌 48 Esplanade
- ⏰ Tues-Sun 10am-5pm; Storyland Wed-Sun 11am-2:30pm
- 💲 museum $6; botanical garden $5; Storyland $2; Carousel Gardens $1 entry, $8 all-day rides
- 🚻 good
- ✕ Museum Courtyard Cafe, Cafe Degas (p. 85)

DON'T MISS
- Haitian art exhibit and decorative arts in the museum • a walk or bike ride around the perimeter • Pavilion of the Two Sisters in the Botanical Garden • a ride on the antique carousel

MISSISSIPPI RIVER

The father of waters is a determined yet meandering artery that's seen more of the USA than most of the country's citizens. Waking up in Minnesota, the river encourages other watercourses to join it on its 2500-mile trip south; through its powers of persuasion, it ultimately drains 41% of the USA. At a particularly dramatic bend, only 160 miles from the Gulf of Mexico, New Orleans built its livelihood off this workhorse.

At first, river travel was slow, with crude hand-hewn barges floated downriver from points north, and sailing ships entering the river from the high seas. The river didn't become a viable highway until the advent of the steamboat, which was developed by Robert Fulton in 1807 and unaffectionately referred to as a sinking volcano. In 1812 the *New Orleans* was launched at a speed of 3mph from Pittsburgh, Pennsylvania. A remarkably short three months later, it was the first steam-powered vessel to reach New Orleans. Within a decade the city's population mushroomed as a result of river traffic. Palatial paddle wheelers also brought entertainment to the river and employed jazz musicians, including a young Louis Armstrong.

The river changes its course like a dancing boxer dodging an anticipated punch. Coaxing the river onto a more reliable path has occupied engineers since 1735, when a 3ft-high levee system was built 30 miles

INFORMATION

✉ foot of the French Quarter

☉ dusk is the prettiest time

✕ Cafe du Monde (p. 72)

The future looks bright aboard the ferry

upstream and 12 miles downstream. The river jumped its banks in the spring of 1927, resulting in government-funded higher levee walls, and later an 8½-mile above-ground floodwall around New Orleans. A total of 22 pumping stations keep New Orleans from filling up like a basin, and every spring, inhabitants watch the river nervously as it silently swells with snowmelt.

DON'T MISS

• a ride on the Canal St ferry (p. 42) • a *Natchez* steamboat river cruise (p. 55) • a stroll along Moonwalk (p. 40) • the Mississippi River exhibit in the Cabildo (p. 32) • educational plaques along Riverwalk (p. 41)

VOODOO IN NEW ORLEANS

Regarded with suspicion, hostility or ridicule, voodoo hasn't enjoyed a flattering reputation in the USA. But in New Orleans, voodoo musters the

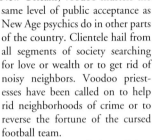

same level of public acceptance as New Age psychics do in other parts of the country. Clientele hail from all segments of society searching for love or wealth or to get rid of noisy neighbors. Voodoo priestesses have been called on to help rid neighborhoods of crime or to reverse the fortune of the cursed football team.

INFORMATION

ⓘ Voodoo Spiritual Temple (828 N Rampart St; ☎ 522-9627; p. 66); Historic Voodoo Museum (724 Dumaine St; ☎ 523-7685; p. 33); Historic New Orleans Walking Tours (☎ 947-2120; p. 54)

                                                                             good

In the African animist tradition, godlike spirits freely interacted with the observable world. As this cosmology traveled from Africa to Haiti and beyond to Louisiana, it merged with varying peoples' rituals and customs to become what is regarded today as voodoo. The gods of voodoo are called *loa* and are arranged in a hierarchy with assigned tasks and bribable tastes. Legba guards the gate between the human and spiritual worlds and can bestow favors to humans in exchange for meats and rum. As pressure grew for slaves to Christianize, Louisiana voodoo adopted Catholic saints as gods and added their statues to revered altars. Voodoo also encompasses the folk traditions of herbal healing; potions (gris-gris) are concocted to heal bones, improve relationships and exact revenge. **Congo Square** (6, F4) served as a gathering place for slaves; a place for staging elaborate African dances, socializing, consulting voodoo doctors and performing rituals.

DON'T MISS
• the albino snake in the Historic Voodoo Museum (p.33) • souvenir hunting at Zombie's House of Voodoo (p. 66) • numbered voodoo potions at the Pharmacy Museum (p. 42)

Shake things up with some voodoo

A marked shift in New Orleans voodoo occurred with the emergence of two controversial figures, Marie Laveau and Dr John. Through theatrics, blackmail and business savvy, they popularized the practice, opened rituals up to whites and gained personal wealth and power. Laveau's beginnings were quite mundane: she was a free woman of color, and hairdresser living in the Quarter. Dr John, however, had a more checkered past: born in Africa (he claimed to be a Senegalese prince), he was enslaved by the Spanish but later earned his freedom and became a sailor. He came to New Orleans in the late 1800s and quickly gained a following as a powerful voodoo doctor.

Both were sought out for their fortune-telling abilities, which relied on paid spies and Laveau's access to her gossiping hairdressing clients rather than divine powers. They also dramatized secret voodoo rituals for white spectators, complete with admission fees and refreshments. The story gets murky regarding Marie Laveau and her daughter of the same name; by some accounts, the elder placed her daughter in the public eye to convince followers that she never aged. One of the Marie Laveaus is buried in St Louis Cemetery No 1, but no one knows which one.

Consult a priestess

To explore the practice consider scheduling a reading or consultation with Priestess Miriam at **Voodoo Spiritual Temple** (6, F5), visiting the **New Orleans Historic Voodoo Museum** (6, F6), or attending the cemetery and voodoo tour of **Historic New Orleans Walking Tours**.

CEMETERIES

New Orleans' love of tradition is most easily demonstrated in its famous cemeteries. These small cities of the dead are traversed by narrow paths between rows of aboveground, boxlike tombs just tall enough to form a maze. Some are pristinely whitewashed, with ornamental roofs. Others have bowed to time, their facades exposing bare brick, and wild grasses, like unwanted hair, have sprouted from the joints.

Most tombs are aboveground, reflecting the Spanish burial tradition and accommodating the area's high water table. The communal tombs, like the living city's ancestral homes, are inherited by the next generation. The interred bodies aren't embalmed and the vaults, which are shaped like ovens, reach decomposing temperatures. This leaves room for the next inhabitant who can be laid to rest a year and a day after the previous burial. All Souls Day is still celebrated in the cemeteries with a festive gathering of family and friends.

The family tomb belongs to one family for burial of successive generations. Wall vaults are typically owned by fraternal organizations, such as benevolent societies or firefighters associations, for burial of their members who may not be able to afford other means; many immigrants were buried this way. The stepped tombs are designed to house only one body.

INFORMATION

- ⊠ St Louis Cemetery No 1 (Basin & Conti Sts), Lafayette Cemetery No 1 (Washington Ave btw Prytania & Coliseum Sts), Metairie Cemetery (Pontchartrain Blvd)
- 🚋 Lafayette Cemetery No 1: St Charles streetcar to Washington Ave
- 🚌 St Louis Cemetery No 1: go with a tour group
- 🚗 Metairie Cemetery: Esplanade Ave toward the lake to City Park Ave and sharp right on to Pontchartrain Blvd after I-10 underpass
- ☉ Lafayette 9am-2:30pm; other cemeteries 9am-4pm
- 💲 free
- ⓘ tours of St Louis by Historic New Orleans (☎ 947-2120); tours of Lafayette by Save our Cemeteries (☎ 525-3377); self-guided audio tours of Metairie from Lakelawn Funeral Home (5100 Pontchartrain Blvd; 2, C6; ☎ 486-6331)

DON'T MISS
- Marie Laveau's tomb and the Italian Mutual Benevolent Society tomb in St Louis No 1 • Millionaire's Row (Aves M and D), the Chapman H Hyams mausoleum and the Moriarty monument in Metairie

Of the 40 cemeteries in New Orleans, **St Louis Cemetery No 1** (6, G3) is the oldest (1789), with tombs outdating most buildings in the French Quarter. With the skyscrapers of the CBD in the background, this decaying boneyard houses voodoo priestess Marie Laveau, Bernard de Marigny (whose plantation was divided up to build Faubourg Marigny) and Homer Adolph Plessy (a complainant in the 1896 Supreme Court case of *Plessy v Ferguson*). The acid trip in *Easy Rider* was filmed here. This cemetery is not safe to wander in alone; joining a tour not only increases safety, it adds to your enjoyment of the cemetery's history.

In the Garden District, **Lafayette Cemetery No 1** (3, F12) contains several tombs that bear Irish and German names; many of the people buried here were killed by the yellow fever epidemics.

The grand **Metairie Cemetery** (2, C6) is as opulent as the mansions that formerly housed the deceased. Replicas of Athenian temples, Egyptian sphinxes and Gothic cathedrals house some of the city's most powerful players.

Be sure to vacate the cemeteries before the witching hour

ST CHARLES STREETCAR (5, C7)

Like an olive green caterpillar, steered by its alert antennas, the St Charles streetcar plots a straight path through the canopied oaks and grassy neutral ground. It's a lovely ride, which can be taken to a specific destination or just for the ramble. Seat yourself on a mahogany bench beside the huge open windows, eavesdrop on your gossiping neighbors, and hold tight as you're pitched forward with a sudden stop to pick up commuters or tourists. Detestable Ignatius J Reilly from *Confederacy of Dunces* rode this route from his Irish Channel home to his hot-dog vending job in the French Quarter.

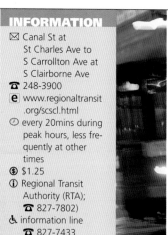

INFORMATION

- ✉ Canal St at St Charles Ave to S Carrollton Ave at S Clairborne Ave
- ☎ 248-3900
- e www.regionaltransit .org/scscl.html
- ⏱ every 20mins during peak hours, less frequently at other times
- $ $1.25
- ⓘ Regional Transit Authority (RTA); ☎ 827-7802)
- ♿ information line ☎ 827-7433

Since 1835, many people have ridden to and fro on this line, which started out as a horse-drawn vehicle called the New Orleans & Carrollton Railroad. In 1893 the horse was replaced with electricity, which is still used today. The line survived the automobile invasion when other streetcar lines were disassembled, and today is the oldest continuously operating line in the country. The fares, however, have increased from a nickel to $1.25; be sure to have exact change.

The introduction of the streetcar allowed New Orleans' residents to move farther from Canal St. The neighborhoods of the Upper Garden District, Uptown and Riverbend were once separate municipalities (Lafayette, Jefferson and Carrollton) and took over former plantations thanks to the streetcars trundling up and down St Charles Ave.

DON'T MISS
- St Charles streetcar tour (p. 48) • getting a window seat
- thanking the driver

sights & activities

New Orleans' major attractions are in the **French Quarter**, which is a compact zone bounded by Canal St, Esplanade Ave, N Rampart St and the river. This is the oldest section with the most foreign influences. It is also the most 'touristified'. The architecture here is utterly charming, and music seems to seep from the drain spouts. You'll easily get trapped within its confines, reluctant to venture beyond Canal St, but do yourself a favor and explore outside of the Quarter for a little perspective.

Downriver from Esplanade Ave is the **Faubourg Marigny**, which melts imperceptibly into the **Bywater**. The Marigny was the mistress zone where Creole gentlemen would purchase homes for their lovers, typically free women of color. The modest cottages have since been adopted by artists and bohemians, who construct huge art projects in their backyards and live quiet lives of supreme eccentricity. Frenchmen St has become a nouveau club zone attracting yuppies and chicsters.

On the upriver side of Canal St, which historically divided the older French Quarter from the younger American sector, is the **Central Business District (CBD)**. Upriver from Poydras St, the once derelict **Warehouse District** is beginning to sprout high-quality art galleries and major tourist draws such as the National D-Day Museum and the new Ogden Museum of Southern Art. At night the neighborhood becomes surprisingly desolate.

Once you cross Hwy 90, you've entered the hip **Lower Garden District**, where wealthy Americans showed the austere Creoles how to spend money. The neighborhood has recently been adopted by coffee-drinking, tattooed youngsters and urban revivalists. Upriver from Jackson Ave is the **Garden District**; it replaced the Lower Garden District in the race to build a bigger and better house and was in turn replaced by **Uptown**, upriver from Louisiana Ave. Audubon Park and Zoo, and Tulane University make Uptown an interesting destination on the St Charles streetcar. Beyond Uptown is the modest neighborhood of **Riverbend**, so named for the river's dramatic turn.

Off the Beaten Track

If you hit New Orleans during its peak, the French Quarter will be one sweaty line – you'll wait for a table at a restaurant, to buy tickets, to walk down Bourbon St and to ride the streetcar. To escape the crowds, rent a bike and hightail it uptown where the pace is slower. Audubon Park is a regenerative green space, where you can ride the paved trails or climb a live oak. If shopping therapy calms the nerves, cruise the funky shops along Magazine St in the Lower Garden District. The huge Canal St ferry has plenty of room for sightseers and offers a glimpse of the wide open spaces of the Mississippi River.

Shopping therapy on Magazine St

MUSEUMS & GALLERIES

Amistad Research Center (3, D4)

The *Amistad* was a small, Cuba-bound schooner illegally transporting Africans to enslavement in 1839. After a mutiny, the schooner was misdirected to New York where the Africans were jailed. A US Supreme Court decision set the Africans free. Named in this event's honor, this is one of the country's largest repositories of African-American historical materials, including books on freemasonry, art and photography.

✉ **Tilton Hall, Tulane University** ☎ **865-5535** **e** **www.tulane.edu/~amistad** ☒ **St Charles at Audubon Park** ⏰ **Mon-Sat 9am-4pm** ⑤ **free**

The Backstreet Museum (6, E5)

'Backstreet' refers literally to the streets in the African-American community outside the surveillance of white authority. It was here that jazz and second-line parades or masking Mardi Gras Indians took over the usual business of the streets. In an old funeral home in Tremé, Sylvester Francis leads tours through his collection of New Orleans African-American memorabilia.

✉ **1116 St Claude Ave** ☎ **525-1733** ☒ **cab or drive** ⏰ **by appointment** ⑤ **donation accepted**

Cabildo (6, G6)

This scattershot collection belonging to the Louisiana State Museum displays artifacts from the city's colonial history with digressions on how the Creoles amused themselves. The centerpiece of the museum is the Napoleon bronze death mask presented to the city by the emperor's bedside doctor. A lock of Andrew Jackson's hair, an iron collar and other odds and ends push the visitor through the Battle of New Orleans to Mississippi River trade and modern times.

✉ **Jackson Sq** ☎ **568-6968** **e** **lsm.crt.state.la.us** ⏰ **Tues-Sat 9am-5pm** ⑤ **$5/4/free** ♿ **good**

Civil War Museum (5, H6)

Claiming to be the oldest museum in the state, the Civil War Museum displays swords, flags and Jefferson Davis memorabilia. Other items crammed into waist-high display cases include personal effects from common soldiers and pieces of Robert E Lee's silver service. The exhibits aren't particularly professional, but building buffs will be intrigued by the Confederate Memorial Hall's terra-cotta arches and interior exposed cypress beams.

✉ **929 Camp St** ☎ **523-4522** ☒ **St Charles at Lee Circle** ⏰ **Mon-Sat 10am-4pm** ⑤ **$5/2**

No, the Cabildo doesn't have an aviary but it does have a Napoleon death mask

Contemporary Arts Center (5, G7)

Within 10,000 sq ft of renovated warehouse space, CAC runs dozens of changing exhibits spotlighting Louisiana artists working in a variety of media. The center's performance space hosts dance and music events, and an education division offers workshops for children.

✉ 900 Camp St
☎ 528-3805 e www.cacno.org 🚊 St Charles at Lee Circle
🕑 Tues-Sun 11am-5pm
$ $5/3 ⅄ good

Historic New Orleans Collection (6, H5)

For a fantastic history lesson, visit the history galleries of this nonprofit organization. A knowledgeable tour guide leads groups through such primary source materials as Iberville's request to establish a colony and Louisiana Purchase documents. Tours of the benefactors' renovated townhouse are also given. The 1st-floor exhibit space is free and celebrates the Louisiana Purchase bicentennial of 2003.

✉ 533 Royal St
☎ 523-4662
e www.hnoc.org
🕑 Tues-Sun 10am-3pm
$ $4 ⅄ good

Historic Voodoo Museum (6, F6)

This small museum has simple but authentic displays of voodoo historical figures, such as Marie Laveau, voodoo altars dedicated to Papa La Bas and the spirit of the Louisiana swamp. A little educational, a little devotional, this collection was founded by Charles Gandolfo, whose grandfather was cured of lockjaw by a voodoo priestess. The 217 N Peters St location has additional exhibits.

✉ 724 Dumaine St
☎ 523-7685 🕑 10am-8pm $ $7/5.50 ⅄ good

Hogan Jazz Archives (3, D5)

Serious jazz researchers will find a wealth of information in this archival library. Recordings of the Original Dixieland Jazz Band in 1917, oral histories and early concert posters can be retrieved by the librarian on request.

✉ Joseph Merrick Jones Hall, Tulane University ☎ 865-5688
🚊 St Charles at Audubon Park 🕑 Mon-Fri 8:30am-5pm, Sat 9:30am-1pm $ free ⅄ good

National D-Day Museum (5, H7)

Although the connection between D-Day and New Orleans seems tenuous, this museum is a top-notch, Smithsonian-quality tour. The top floors trace the history of WWII with documentary style, using personal stories to humanize the facts. The 1st floor honors Higgins Industries, the New Orleans–based boat builder contracted to develop amphibious landing vehicles. Modified versions of crafts used by trappers and the oil industry, Higgins' shallow draft boats were used to storm the beaches at Normandy on that fateful day.

✉ 945 Camp St
☎ 527-6012
e www.ddaymuseum.org 🚊 St Charles at Lee Circle 🕑 9am-5pm
$ $10/5 ⅄ good

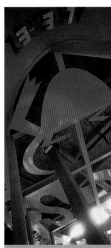

Contemporary Arts Center

Newcomb Art Gallery/Woldenberg Art Center (3, C5)

The Newcomb College was founded in 1886 to provide women with a liberal arts education. A coordinate division of Tulane University, Newcomb became most famous for its Arts and Crafts–style pottery. Female students weren't allowed to throw their own pots and many famous male potters, including George Orr, were employed for the dirty work. Traveling exhibits and student-produced artwork can be viewed at the gallery.

✉ Broadway & Willow Sts, Tulane campus ☎ 865-5328 e www.tulane.edu/~newcomb/artindex.html 🚋 St Charles at Broadway ⏰ Mon-Fri 10am-5pm, Sat-Sun noon-5pm $ free ♿ good

New Orleans African American Museum of Art, Culture & History (6, D4)

In a fine Creole villa, the New Orleans African American Museum of Art, Culture & History exhibits rotating and traveling shows of African-American art. Displays have included handmade masks and dioramas of 'dream houses' from local school children. The museum is in the Tremé, a neighborhood where free people of color owned property prior to the Civil War.

✉ 1418 Governor Nicholls St ☎ 565-7497 e www.noaam.org 🚕 cab or drive ⏰ Mon-Fri 10am-5pm, Sat 10am-2pm $ $5/2

Created by New Orleans artist Richard Thomas' Pieces of Power Artist Youth Group

New Orleans Jazz National Historic Park (6, G7)

The name implies something more compelling than a National Park Service center. But grand plans to move the center to Louis Armstrong Park are slowly unfolding. When they are realized, the park will become a cultural center for the city that birthed jazz. The center does host music events.

✉ 916 N Peters St ☎ 877-520-0677 e www.nps.gov/neor ⏰ 9am-5pm $ free ♿ good

Ogden Museum of Southern Art (5, G6)

The Ogden Museum, recently associated with the Smithsonian Institution, is a premier showcase of Southern art. Through folk art, modern painting, traditional crafts and poignant photography, the South speaks fluently about itself and its struggles. A much-heralded site on Camp St will become the museum's new home sometime before the end of 2004; until then a temporary gallery is at 603 Julia St (5,G6).

✉ 603 Julia St ☎ 539-9600 e www.ogdenmuseum.org 🚋 St Charles at Lee Circle ⏰ Tues-Sun 10am-5pm $ donation for temporary gallery; call for admission prices for new location

Presbytère (6, G6)

The Mardi Gras exhibit at the Presbytère is a must-see for Fat Tuesday regulars and novices. Elaborate costumes, video footage and piped music create a dynamic carnival energy, even within the sterile halls of a state museum. Crown jewels from the old-line krewes, famous throws and doubloons, and climb-aboard floats attempt to catalog the immense cultural history of this home-grown festival.

✉ Jackson Sq ☎ 568-6968 e lsm.crt.state.la.us ⏰ Tues-Sun 9am-5pm $ $5 ♿ good

HISTORIC HOMES & NOTABLE BUILDINGS

Beauregard-Keyes House Museum

(6, F7) Someday you should be so lucky as to leave your name to a former residence. General PGT Beauregard, a Louisiana native and commander of the Civil War's first shots, lived in this 1826 Greek revival house for only 18 months. The longer resident was Francis Parkinson Keyes, an author of over 51 novels, including *Dinner at Antoine's* (1948). Period pieces decorate the main house, while Keyes' doll and decorative ceramic collections occupy the back cottage.

✉ **1113 Chartres St** ☎ **523-7257** ⏲ **tours on the hr Mon-Sat 10am-3pm** ⑤ **$5/2**

Cornstalk Hotel

(6, F6) The cast-iron fence enclosing this B&B spawns grand stories. Some say the painted cornstalk motif was ordered for a homesick bride from Iowa by her New Orleans husband. The know-it-all historians, however, maintain that the design was a popular 1859 catalog order and has no sentimental connection to Midwest cornfields.

✉ **915 Royal St**

Degas House **(4, H5)**

The impressionist painter Edgar Degas came to New Orleans for four months in 1872 to visit his Creole cousins. During his visit he completed 18 paintings and four sketches, the most famous of which is *A Cotton Office in New Orleans*. The tour introduces visitors to the period and the family members portrayed in the painter's New Orleans paintings.

✉ **2306 Esplanade** ☎ **821-5009** e **www .degashouse.com** 🚌 **48 Esplanade at N Tonti St** ⏲ **by appointment; 1hr tour** ⑤ **$10/5**

1850 House Museum

(6, G6) In the lower Pontalba Building, this row house, a property of the state museum, replicates the way a middle-class family might have lived. The self-guided tour views the period-decorated rooms, many of them no bigger than your closet-sized hotel rooms.

✉ **523 St Ann St** ☎ **568-6968** e **lsm.crt .state.la.us** ⏲ **Tues-Sun 9am-5pm** ⑤ **$3/2**

Factors Row **(5, D6)**

In the late 1800s the city's booming cotton trade centered on Carondelet in the American sector. Degas painted *A Cotton Office in New Orleans* while visiting his uncle's office here in 1873.

✉ **806 Perdido St**

Faulkner House

(6, G6) In 1925 the French Quarter was a slum, discarded by the wealthy and desperately adopted by poor immigrants. This was the year that William Faulkner rented an apartment overlooking the garden behind St Louis Cathedral. While living in the city he described as a 'courtesan, not old and yet no longer young,' Faulkner worked for the *Times-Picayune* and published his first novel, *Soldier's Pay* (1926). The building is now one of the city's finest bookstores (p. 67).

✉ **624 Pirate's Alley** ☎ **524-2940** ⏲ **10am-6pm** ⑤ **free**

Gallier Hall **(5, E6)**

Gallier Hall served as the city hall from 1853 to 1957. The imposing Greek revival structure overlooking Lafayette Square was designed by famed architect James Gallier Sr at a derisive time in New Orleans' history. Americans were made to feel unwelcome in the Vieux Carré by the older Creole society, but Yankee ingenuity was fueling a booming economy.

✉ **545 St Charles Ave** 🚃 **St Charles at Lafayette Sq**

Leave the light on for me at the Cornstalk Hotel

Storyville

Like every rough and tumble port city, New Orleans had (*correction,* has) prostitution. The brothels were so popular that even the politicians publicly acknowledged their existence. In an attempt to regulate the trade, city official Sidney Story proposed a legalized but contained red-light district in 1897 to occupy the lakeside portion of the French Quarter. A modern-day Gomorrah flourished and adopted the do-gooder's name, Storyville. Pimps, madames, drug pushers and moonlighting musicians caroused in this fabled city. Jazz is said to have sprung from its dens, where the classical pianos and horns were ragged with lusty expression. The district was finally closed down in 1917 by navy orders to protect young recruits. To further erase the legend, the houses were razed in 1940 and a housing project erected in their place.

Gallier House Museum (6, F7)

Many of New Orleans' Greek revival buildings were designed by James Gallier Sr and James Gallier Jr. The son built this technologically advanced house in 1857, complete with indoor plumbing and a flush toilet. In summer, the rooms are given seasonal 'dress:' coverings and netting that protected the inhabitants and furnishings from the elements. There are also intact slave quarters.

✉ 1118-1132 Royal St
☎ 525-5661
e www.gnofn.org
🕐 Mon-Fri 10am-3:30pm 💲 $6/5

Hermann-Grima House (6, G4)

More New England than Creole, this Federal-style house was built in 1831 by Samuel Hermann, a Jewish entrepreneur. Because of financial hardship, Hermann sold it to Felix Grima, a lawyer. The Quarter's only surviving horse stable remains on the property. Traditional open-hearth cooking demonstrations are held for the public on Thursdays.

✉ 820 St Louis St
☎ 525-5661 e www.gnofn.org/~hggh
🕐 Mon-Fri 10am-3:30pm 💲 $6/5

Hibernia National Bank (5, D6)

This major banking headquarters anchors the area once called 'bankers row.' The name Hibernia indicates the bank's German heritage. Sadly, they don't give out free money to curious visitors.

✉ 812 Gravier St
🕐 Mon-Fri 10am-3pm, Sat 10am-noon 💲 free

Labranche Building (6, G6)

Like a veiled maiden, the 1840s Labranche building is draped with ornate cast-iron work bearing a pattern of leafy tree branches pregnant with acorns. It is said that the tree motif corresponds to the first owner's last name, Labranche. This is a gallicized version of the family's paternal name, Zweig, which in German means 'twig.'

✉ 700 Royal St

LeMonnier Mansion (6, G5)

Known as the first skyscraper in New Orleans, the LeMonnier Mansion was built in 1811 and grew to four stories by 1876. Dr Yves LeMonnier, the owner in 1811, left his initials 'YLM' in the wrought-iron balcony – an artistic form of tagging.

✉ 640 Royal St

Longue Vue House & Gardens

Near the Metairie Cemetery, Longue Vue was built in the 1940s by philanthropists Edith and Edgar Stern. Most remarkable are the eight acres of gardens, including a formal Spanish garden, wild forest and children's garden.

✉ 7 Bamboo Rd
☎ 488-5488 e www.longuevue.com
♿ drive 🕐 Mon-Sat 10am-4:30pm, Sun 1-5pm 💲 $7/3

Louisiana State Bank (6, H5)

This imposing structure was designed in 1820 by Benjamin Henry Latrobe, the architect of the south wing of the US Capitol. Notice the bank's monograms (LSB) in the ironwork balcony.

✉ 403 Royal St

Gallier House Museum

Madame John's Legacy (6, G6)

The architecture and folk-art exhibit are the most interesting aspects of this historic property of the state museum. Built in West Indies style, the 1st floor is made of brick and was used for storage, much like a basement. The living quarters were on the 2nd floor, which is made of wood. Notice the cigar-shaped columns on the exterior balcony. George Washington Cable's short story *Tite Poulette*, about a quadroon known as Madame John, was set in this house.

- ✉ **632 Dumaine St**
- ☎ **568-6968**
- 🖥 **lsm.crt.state.la.us**
- ⏰ **Tues-Sun 9am-5pm**
- 💲 **$3/2** ♿ **good**

Maspero's Exchange (6, H5)

A plaque marks the spot of Pierre Maspero's slave auction and coffeehouse – a chilling combination from a modern perspective. The Exchange was selected as a headquarters for the local militia hastily assembled to aid Andrew Jackson in the fight against the advancing British army; the forces met on the battlegrounds of Chalmette, three years after the war of 1812 officially ended.

- ✉ **440 Chartres St**

New Orleans Cotton Exchange (5, D6)

A group of merchants and bankers organized the Cotton Exchange in 1871 to regulate prices and centralize trading. The building standing here today is the third exchange house built on this site and the last to have hosted commodity exchanges.

- ✉ **231 Carondelet St**

Check out the family crystal at the Pitot House Museum

Peychaud's Pharmacy (6, H5)

Back when apothecaries let blood and sold voodoo potions, AA Peychaud, a French refugee from Haiti, earned a place in Quarter lore with his distinctive cure-all. For his ailing customers, he mixed his patented bitters recipe (known today as Peychaud's Bitters) with sweeter liquors in a double-sided egg cup known as a *coquetier*, eventually rendered as 'cocktail.' An antique gun shop now occupies the apothecary.

- ✉ **437 Royal St**

Pitot House Museum (4, G3)

Designed to encourage air circulation, Creole houses typically have double-pitched roofs with dormer windows, louvered-shuttered doors and interior rooms that open into each other (without a main corridor). This 1799 French-colonial plantation house is an excellent example of the style and takes its name from James Pitot, the first mayor of the incorporated city of New Orleans.

- ✉ **1440 Moss St**
- ☎ **482-0312** 🚌 **48 Esplanade to Moss St**
- ⏰ **Wed-Sat 10am-3pm**
- 💲 **$5/3**

Ursuline Convent (6, F7)

The French order of Ursuline nuns came to New Orleans in the 1700s to educate the colony's girls and to operate a small hospital. A convent was built for them by the French Colonial Army in 1752, making this the oldest building in the Mississippi Valley. The convent survived the city's fires thanks to concerted firefighting efforts by the citizenry. The sisters' devotionals were credited with helping Jackson win the Battle of New Orleans.

- ✉ **1100 Chartres St**
- ☎ **529-3040** ⏰ **tours on the hr Tues-Fri 10am-3pm (except noon), Sat-Sun 11:15am, 1pm & 2pm**
- 💲 **$5/2** ♿ **good**

US Customs House (6, J5)

Closed to the public, the US Customs House first housed government offices in 1856, some seven years after the cornerstone had been laid. Prior to the Civil War, PGT Beauregard oversaw construction. During the Reconstruction period, the African-American division of the Republican party had its offices here. The marble hall on the 2nd floor is said to be stunning.

- ✉ **423 Canal St**

UNIVERSITIES & COLLEGES

Dillard University

(2, B8) Historically black, Dillard University was founded in 1869 by the Congregational Church. Offering a liberal arts education, Dillard is especially recognized for its visual arts program. The stately Avenue of Oaks draws many visitors.
✉ **2601 Gentilly Blvd**
☎ **283-8822** |e| **www .dillard.edu** 🚗 **cab or drive** ♿ **good**

Loyola University

(3, D5) The largest Catholic university in the South, Loyola was founded by the Jesuits in 1904. The school's McDermott Memorial Church and Holy Name of Jesus Church are both open to visitors.
✉ **6363 St Charles Ave**
☎ **865-3240** |e| **www .loyno.edu** 🚈 **St Charles at Audubon Park** ♿ **good**

Tulane University

(3, D5) Tulane University was founded in 1834 as the South's first medical school in order to control the region's epidemics of cholera and yellow fever. A law school and collegiate departments were added later. The gray-stone campus makes for a nice walk, and the excellent Newcomb Art Gallery (p. 34), Amistad Research Center (p. 32) and Hogan Jazz Archives (p. 33) welcome visitors.
✉ **6839 St Charles Ave**
☎ **865-4000** |e| **www .tulane.edu** 🚈 **St Charles at Audubon Park** ♿ **good**

Loyola University

Xavier University

(4, J1) The only historically black Catholic university in the country, Xavier was founded in 1915 by the Sisters of the Blessed Sacrament. The school's college of pharmacy is well respected.
✉ **1 Drexel Dr** ☎ **486-7411** |e| **www.xula.edu** 🚗 **cab or drive** ♿ **good**

Leaning toward higher education? Visit Tulane University

PLACES OF WORSHIP

Christ Church Cathedral (3, F12)

Although Protestants have lived in New Orleans since colonial times, there were no established churches until 1805. An ad in the *Louisiana Gazette* invited Protestants to form a congregation, resulting in Christ Church, which by popular vote became Episcopalian. The present church was built in 1886.

⊠ **2919 St Charles Ave**
☎ **895-6602** 🚊 **St Charles at Sixth St**
🕐 **Sun services 7:30am, 9am & 11am**
⑤ **donation accepted**
♿ **good**

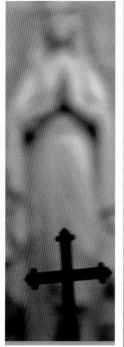

St Augustine's

St Expedite

The popular legend about New Orleans' unofficial patron saint, St Expedite, demonstrates the city's true creativity, unhindered by the rigors of canonization, and its ability to spin a good yarn. In an unnamed year, a crate packed with statues of saints was delivered to an order of New Orleans nuns. They came across a box marked *'spedito'*, which they took to mean 'rush' in Italian. Inside was a figurine of what looked like a Roman general, but the nuns had never met this saint. In the spirit of charity, they gave the statue a home on the altar and named him St Expedite, assigning him the job of finding prompt solutions. Being that New Orleans is an insular island, St Expedite was soon regarded as the nuns' own creation, never mind that he has been the patron saint of Sicily since the 1700s and that Paris nuns tell a similar creation myth.

Our Lady of Guadeloupe Church

(6, G3) During the 1853 yellow fever epidemic, the city struggled to bury the victims within Catholic strictures and used this chapel as a mortuary. It was rechristened Our Lady of Guadeloupe in 1931. Of the church's patrons saints, there are St Jude, impossible cases; St Michael, police; St Florian, firefighters; and St Expedite, to hurry things up.

⊠ **411 N Rampart St**
☎ **525-1551** 🕐 **open 7am-6pm** ⑤ **donation accepted** ♿ **good**

St Augustine's (6, E5)

The second oldest African-American Catholic Church in the country, St Augustine's opened in 1842. The Sisters of the Holy Family, an order of black Creole nuns, are depicted in a panel of the church's stained-glass windows. Jazz funerals frequently depart from the church, and pass through the streets of the Tremé en route to the cemetery.

⊠ **1210 Governor Nicholls St** ☎ **525-5934** 🚕 **cab or drive**
🕐 **Sun mass 10am** ⑤ **donation accepted** ♿ **good**

St Patrick's Church

(5, F7) The Irish immigrants of the 1830s established this parish church, one of many in the city that ministered to the recently arrived Europeans. Locals joke that this is where God speaks English.

⊠ **724 Camp St**
☎ **525-4413** 🇪 **www .oldstpatricks.org** 🚊 **St Charles at Girod St** 🕐 **Sun mass 8am, 9:30am & 11am**
⑤ **donation accepted** ♿ **good**

PARKS & GARDENS

Audubon Park (3, E4)
Incorporate a stroll through this 400-acre park during a visit to the Audubon Zoo. Between the streetcar stop on St Charles Ave and the zoo, a mile-long paved path circles a lagoon teeming with birdlife. Egrets perch on gnarled live oaks, whose boughs dip toward the murky water, for a vain glimpse of their reflection.
✉ **bounded by St Charles Ave, Magazine St, Exposition Blvd & Walnut St** 🚋 **St Charles at Audubon Park**

Lafayette Square
(5, E7) Originally named Place Gravier, this public square was renamed after Lafayette's visit to New Orleans in 1825. It was the gathering place for the American sector of town. Today it hosts free music concerts.
✉ **bounded by St Charles Ave, N & S Maestri & Camp Sts** 🚋 **St Charles at Lafayette Sq**

Spanish Moss
The tangled hairlike plants known as Spanish moss make their homes in the branches of the live oaks in the city's parks. *Tillandsia usneoides* is actually a member of the pineapple family. The French called it 'Spanish beard,' and the Spanish countered by calling it 'French wig.'

Lee Circle (5, H6)
At the center of this roundabout is a statue of Confederate general Robert E Lee facing north, arms crossed, waiting for the Union's next move. The circle was dedicated to the Confederacy after the Civil War in 1884, as a backlash against the Reconstruction period.
🚋 **St Charles at Lee Circle**

Louis Armstrong Park (6, F4)
Named in honor of New Orleans' famous jazz cornetist, Louis Armstrong Park occupies a green stretch between the French Quarter and the Tremé. Inside the festive arched entrance is Congo Square, a historic gathering place for slaves; a statue of Louis Armstrong;

a bust of Sidney Bechet, a New Orleans–born clarinetist; the radio station WWOZ; and cultural and performing arts centers.
✉ **entrance at N Rampart St & St Ann St** 🕐 **daytime only** ♿ **good**

Moonwalk Park
(6, G7) From Jackson Square, cross Decatur St toward the river. Climb the stairs to the viewing platform for a picture-postcard view of the square and St Louis Cathedral. Closer to the river is a wide promenade giving an unhindered view of the gigantic container ships forging along the muddy Mississippi. The 'father of rivers' gets better looking every year.
✉ **river side of Jackson Sq**

From brass to bronze: Satchmo is immortalized at Louis Armstrong Park

Audubon Park

Riverwalk (5, F10)
Behind the huge Riverwalk mall, facing the river, this pleasant walkway is lined with informative plaques about the advent and death of river trade and steamboat jazz bands. When the city was founded, this portion was underwater.
✉ **entrance at Poydras St** 🚇 **Riverfront at Riverwalk Mall**

Woldenberg Riverfront Park (6, K6)
Between the river and the aquarium, this green space used to be lined with wharves and the activity of loading or unloading bales of cotton, barrels of sugar and bunches of bananas. Now the park hosts concerts, evening strolls and departure points for riverboat cruises.
✉ **river side of aquarium**

COOKING CLASSES

Cookin' Cajun Cooking School
(5, F10) Jambalaya, shrimp Creole and bananas Foster are just some of the specialties that might appear on the menu for this 2hr cooking demonstration. The class exam consists of sampling the prepared dishes. Cookin' Cajun is in the Creole Delicacies Gourmet Shop in the Riverwalk Mall.
✉ **1 Poydras St, Riverwalk Mall** ☎ 586-8832 **e** www.cookin cajun.com 🚇 **Riverfront at Riverwalk Mall** ⏰ **class times vary** ⑤ **$20** ♿ **good**

New Orleans School of Cooking (6, H5)
A lot of humor and a dash of attitude get stirred into the pot during this 3hr cooking demonstration. Participants get to eat the lesson plan of gumbo, jambalaya, bread pudding and pralines, washed down with an Abita beer.
✉ **524 St Louis St** ☎ 525-2665 **e** www .neworleansschoolof cooking.com ⏰ **10am-1pm** ⑤ **$25** ♿ **good**

Learn to cook some one-pot wonders

QUIRKY NEW ORLEANS

Canal St Ferry (6, K6)
Aboard this state-run ferry, you can take a free ride from New Orleans across the river to the west bank suburb of Algiers. If it wasn't for the hum of the ferry's motor, you might swear the river did all the work.

✉ **foot of Canal St at Mississippi River** ◷ **5:45am-midnight, on the hour and the half-hour** ⑤ **free** ₺ **good**

Harrah's New Orleans (5, E9)
This national gaming chain is another glossy anchor in the redevelopment of the old riverfront area. With a faux Mardi Gras theme, Harrah's proudly pushes the standard array of casino bells and whistles, with tables and slots, complimentary drinks and bargain buffets.

✉ **Canal & N Peters Sts** ☎ **800-427-7247** ℮ **www.harrahs.com** ⊠ **Riverfront at Canal St** ◷ **24hrs** ⑤ **free** ₺ **good**

J&M Music Shop
(6, F5) Now Hula Mae's Laundromat, the former J&M Music Shop is where R&B legends such as Fats Domino and Dave Bartholomew recorded in the 1950s. A makeshift exhibit of historic photos can be found inside near the dryers.

✉ **840 Rampart St** ☎ **522-1336** ◷ **10am-9pm** ⑤ **free**

New Orleans Pharmacy Museum
(6, H5) Without even meaning to, you might actually learn something at this relic of a 19th-century pharmacy. Leeches swimming in an enclosed jar greet visitors and instruments of torture sit silently in display cases. Dusty voodoo potions occupy another shelf. Upstairs exhibits explain the scientific aspects of the city's multiple epidemics.

✉ **514 Chartres St** ☎ **565-8027** ℮ **www.pharmacymuseum.org** ◷ **Tues-Sat 10am-5pm** ⑤ **$2/1**

Watch out for leeches at the Pharmacy Museum

Royal Pharmacy
(6, F6) In a quiet part of Royal St, this 100-year-old pharmacy is an uncluttered space where prescriptions are filled and packs of gum are sold. Its notoriety comes from the perfectly preserved 1950s soda fountain that peacefully rests along the back wall, no longer of service to sugar-jacked teens.

✉ **1101 Royal St** ☎ **523-5401** ◷ **Mon-Sat 9am-5pm** ⑤ **free**

Plug away at the slots at Harrah's

KEEPING FIT

New Orleans isn't a workout kind of town, unless you classify moving from one air-conditioned place to another air-conditioned place as exercise. A jogger spotted in the French Quarter causes more of a stir than a bare-breasted Mardi Gras reveler. Ask a local where they workout, and they just giggle. You can get rid of that fried-food hangover with an evening stroll through the Quarter or shaking your tail feathers at a late-night music club. Joggers are spotted on the grassy neutral ground of the St Charles streetcar (run facing oncoming cars, so you can step out of the way). Although mentioned only in whispers, there are several gyms and sports centers that attract the odd weight-conscious local.

Audubon Golf Club
(3, F4) Chase that little white ball around the 18-hole green at Audubon Park. Lots of birdlife and picturesque trees will liven up a bad round.
✉ **473 Walnut St**
☎ **865-8260** e **www .auduboninstitute.org** 🚃 **St Charles at Audubon Park** ⏲ **call for tee times** ⑤ **$12/8 weekdays/weekends**

Bayou Oaks Golf Facility
(4, C3)
This is the largest municipal golf course in the South; it has four 18-hole courses as well as a driving range.
✉ **City Park** ☎ **483-9396** e **www.new orleanscitypark.com** 🚌 **48 Esplanade at City Park** ⏲ **sunup to sundown** ⑤ **$10-18**

Cascade Stables
(3, G3) Horses for riding through Audubon Park are available at Cascade Stables. Introductory lessons are also given for $20 extra.
✉ **6500 Magazine St** ☎ **891-2246** 🚌 **11 Magazine at Audubon Park** ⏲ **9am-5pm** ⑤ **$20/hr**

City Park Riding Stables
(4, C3)
Lessons for groups and individuals are given at the City Park Riding Stables. Riders must be older than six years old and wear hard-soled boots.
✉ **1001 Filmore Ave** ☎ **483-9398** e **www.neworleans citypark.com** 🚌 **48 Esplanade at Filmore Ave** ⏲ **Mon-Fri 9am-7pm, Sat-Sun 9am-5pm** ⑤ **$75/hr; groups $30/person/hr**

City Park Tennis Center
(4, F2)
With 24 hard courts and 10 clay courts, City Park's tennis courts keep the racket crowd happy. Women's and men's locker rooms are on-site. Rentals are available.
✉ **Victory & Anseman Aves, City Park** ☎ **483-9383** e **www.newor leanscitypark.com** 🚌 **48 Esplanade at City Park** ⏲ **Mon-Thur 7am-10pm, Fri-Sun 7am-7pm** ⑤ **$5.50/hr**

Downtown Fitness Center
(6, K5)
Stay pumped at this centrally located gym catering to out-of-towners.

Aerobics, yoga and swimming pools are available.
✉ **380 Canal St, Canal Place** ☎ **525-2956** e **www.downtown fitnesscenter.com** ⏲ **Mon-Fri 6am-9pm** ⑤ **$30/3 days** ♿ **good**

Mackie Shilstone's Pro Spa
(3, E13)
On the 2nd floor of the Avenue Plaza Hotel, this full-service spa and gym attracts some serious gym rats. The full-service salon can aid those afraid of sweat.
✉ **2111 St Charles Ave** ☎ **566-1212** 🚃 **St Charles at Josephine St** ⏲ **Mon-Fri 6am-9pm, Sat-Sun 8am-5pm** ⑤ **$5/day** ♿ **good**

City Park Riding Stables

NEW ORLEANS FOR CHILDREN

Audubon Aquarium of the Americas

(5, E10) All sorts of fish of the sea make an appearance at this cool, shiny aquarium covering aquatic life from North and South America. Menacing sharks, rainforest fish bigger than New York City apartments, sea dragons resembling floating weeds – all silently survey their watery homes. Is a starfish spiny? Visit one of the touch pools to find out. During the school year, the aquarium is quieter in the afternoon; during the summer, the morning hours are best. Combination tickets with the zoo, IMAX theater and Zoo Cruise are available.
✉ 1 Canal St ☎ 581-4629, 800-774-7394
℮ www.auduboninstitute.org ☽ Sun-Thurs 9:30am-6pm, Fri-Sat 9:30am-7pm ⑤ $14/6.50 ⅋ good

Audubon Louisiana Nature Center

About 20mins east of New Orleans, the Louisiana Nature Center occupies a patch of swamp where visitors can meet the local ecology and wildlife. An onsite museum has hands-on exhibits and cares for orphaned or injured animals. Raised platforms wind through a hardwood bottomland forest. A laser light show is offered at weekends at the center's planetarium.
✉ 5601 Read Blvd
☎ 246-7827 ℮ www.auduboninstitute.org
🚗 car ☽ Tues-Fri 9am-5pm, Sat 10am-5pm, Sun noon-5pm
⑤ $5/3 ⅋ good

Audubon Zoological Gardens (3, G3)

The zoo is touted as one of the best in the world. Unfortunately, New Orleans' heat isn't conducive to animal antics. If you don't arrive early on a cool day, you might end up staring at

> ### Monkey Hill
> Excluding the Mississippi Levee, New Orleans' highest landmass is Monkey Hill, inside the Audubon Zoo. Monkey Hill was built in 1933 as part of a federal works project to give New Orleans children the experience of 'elevation.' Once you're acclimated to New Orleans' flat geography, the 27½-ft hill seems quite monstrous and its modest view is breathtaking.

empty exhibits. The zoo is divided into creatively landscaped sections. The Central America section, which houses jaguars, is connected by narrow paths littered with faux Mayan sculptures; elephants inhabit the Asian exhibit with knockoff Khmer ruins. But the most entertaining is the Louisiana Swamp exhibit, decorated with rusty cars and spotlight-loving raccoons.
✉ 6500 Magazine St
☎ 861-2537 ℮ www.auduboninstitute.org
🚊 St Charles at Audubon Park to free shuttle bus 🚢 Zoo Cruise from Aquarium of the Americas ☽ Mon-Fri 9am-4:30pm, Sat-Sun 9am-5pm ⑤ $9/4.75 ⅋ good

Audubon Zoo – Froot Loops, anyone?

Blaine Kern's Mardi Gras World

Blaine Kern's studio artists have been making Mardi Gras floats since 1947. Tours through the warehouse studio visit artists working on next year's floats, which are made of Styrofoam and papier mâché, and parade mainstays, like the 240-ft long float with tens of thousands of fiber-optic lights.
✉ 233 Newton St, Algiers ☎ 361-7821 ℮ www.mardigras world.com 🚢 Canal St ferry to free shuttle bus ⏱ 9:30am-5pm ⑧ $13.50/6.50

Louisiana Children's Museum (5, G7)

What a fun place! There's a big bubble maker and a grocery store with plastic foodstuffs and play cash registers. There's a café with a toy kitchen, where kids cook up plastic dishes to serve to their parents. Kids can pretend to be news anchors. Or fix a flat tire. Are you beat yet? Your children aren't.
✉ 420 Julia St ☎ 523-1357 ℮ www.lcm.org ⏱ Tues-Sat 9:30am-4:30pm, Sun noon-4:30pm ⑧ $6 ⅛ good

Musée Conti Wax Museum (6, H4)

What's better than reading about history? Seeing the historical players rendered in wax. Heroes, emperors and even monsters are always watching you out of the corner of their eyes. And who knew that Napoleon liked to sign away large tracts of land from the comfort of his bathtub?
✉ 917 Conti St

Babysitting Services

Most major hotels – including the W, the Fairmont, Hotel Inter-Continental, the Ritz-Carlton and Le Meridien – offer on-site babysitting services as well as swimming pools and extra bedding for children. If you need to stow the youngsters for a few hours, consider inquiring about these services when making hotel reservations.

☎ 525-2605 ℮ www.get-waxed.com ⏱ 10am-5:30pm ⑧ $6.75/5.75 ⅛ good

Zoo Cruise (5, E10)

Departing from the Aquarium of the Americas dock near the French Quarter, the *John James Audubon* Zoo Cruise delivers passengers to Audubon Landing, near the zoo's Australian Outback exhibit; combination tickets are available for the cruise, zoo and aquarium.
☎ 586-8777 ℮ www .neworleanssteam boat.com ⏱ departs from aquarium 10am, noon, 2pm & 4pm ⑧ round trip $16/8 ⅛ good

Aquarium of the Americas – who's looking at who?

out & about

TOURS
French Quarter

This tour is a sampler of Spanish, French and American architecture. Start at Jackson Square. Go downriver on Chartres St to Dumaine St and turn left to Madame John's Legacy ❶, 632 Dumaine St, an example of French plantation style. Backtrack to Chartres and head towards Ursuline Ave. Ursuline Convent ❷, 1114 Chartres St, is the Quarter's oldest structure, dating to 1749. Take Ursuline Ave to Royal St and turn left; the Cornstalk Hotel ❸, 915 Royal St, is named for its 1859 cornstalk-motif fence. In the 800 block of Royal St, notice the oval

SIGHTS & HIGHLIGHTS
Madame John's Legacy (p. 37)
Ursuline Convent (p. 37)
Cornstalk Hotel (p. 35)
Labranche Building (p. 36)
LeMonnier Mansion (p. 36)
Peychaud's Pharmacy (p. 37)
Louisiana State Bank (p. 36)
Napoleon House (p. 76)

distance 1 mile   **duration** 1hr
▶ **start** St Ann & Chartres Sts
● **end** St Peter & Chartres Sts

Napoleon House

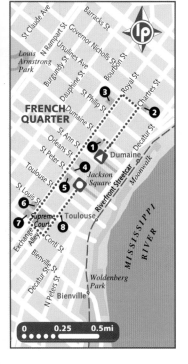

coverings along the building foundations: these are 'weep' holes for air circulation. Continue to the Labranche Building ❹, 700 Royal St, and its photogenic balconies. Stop at the LeMonnier Mansion ❺, No 640, to pick out the initials in the cast-iron work. The cocktail was invented at Peychaud's Pharmacy ❻, No 437. Louisiana State Bank ❼, No 403, is an American adaptation of original Spanish styles. Turn left at Conti St and go past Exchange Alley, once home to famous fencing masters. Turn left on Chartres St to Napoleon House ❽, 500 Chartres St, named in honor of the French emperor. From here Jackson Square is two blocks downriver.

Garden District

During New Orleans' golden age, wealthy Americans built Greek revival mini-plantations upriver from the old French Quarter. Take the streetcar from Canal St to Jackson Ave and head toward the river. At 1410 Jackson Ave, the Greek-columned Buckner House ❶ was built for a cotton merchant in 1856. Turn right on to Chestnut for two blocks, then left onto First St. At 1239 First St, novelist Anne Rice lives in Rosegate ❷, named for its rose-motif cast-iron fence. Continue left for one block to the corner with Camp St. In 1889, Confederate President Jefferson Davis died at Payne-Strachan House ❸, 1134 First St. Backtrack on First St to No 2343 Prytania St, where Louise S McGehee School occupies an 1872 renaissance mansion ❹ designed by James Freret. Turn left to the

SIGHTS & HIGHLIGHTS

Lafayette Cemetery No 1 (p. 29)
Commander's Palace (p. 82)

Commander's Palace

outdoor chapel ❺ of Our Lady of Perpetual Help, 2521 Prytania St. At No 2605, James Gallier designed 1849 Charles Briggs House ❻, unique for its Gothic windows and Elizabethan chimneys. At the corner with Prytania St, Colonel Short's Villa ❼ at 1448 Fourth St is guarded by a cornstalk fence – look closer for morning glories, pumpkins and wheat. Continue to Washington Ave; turn left to explore Lafayette Cemetery No 1 ❽ and have a meal at Commander's Palace ❾, or right to catch the streetcar downtown.

distance 1 mile   **duration** 1½hrs
▶ **start** 🚊 St Charles Ave at Jackson Ave
⏺ **end** 🚊 St Charles Ave at Washington Ave

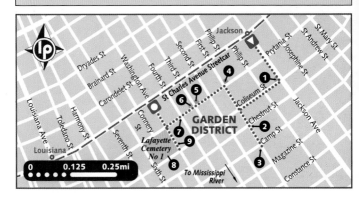

St Charles Streetcar

From the comfort of a window seat on the St Charles streetcar, you can tour New Orleans' uptown neighborhoods. At Canal and Carondelet Sts, catch the streetcar heading uptown. At Lafayette Square, the Greek revival building on the left at No 545 is Gallier Hall ❶, the former city hall. Just past the roundabout, named Lee Circle ❷ in honor of the Confederate general, begins the Garden District. On the right at Sixth St, Christ Church Cathedral ❸ was built in 1886 to serve the city's Protestant inhabitants. At Louisiana Ave, you cross into Uptown District, where the mansions get grander. For a quick drink, hop off at The Columns Hotel ❹, No 3811. Nearby streets (Austerlitz, Constantinople, Marengo, Milan and Jena) celebrate Napoleonic victories. Sacred Heart Academy ❺, a

girls' school, is on the right at Jena St. On the left at Soniat St, the Neo-Italianate mansion ❻ now houses a branch of the public library. On the right at No 5809 is a gorgeous mansion known as the Wedding Cake House ❼. Loyola ❽ and Tulane ❾ Universities approach on the right after Calhoun St. Across the street is Audubon Park ❿. Hop off the streetcar at S Carrollton Ave for a bite at Camellia Grill ⓫; catch the streetcar going the opposite direction to return.

---

distance 12 miles (19km) round trip   **duration** 3hrs
▶ **start** 🚋 Carondelet & Canal Sts
● **end** 🚋 Carondelet & Canal Sts

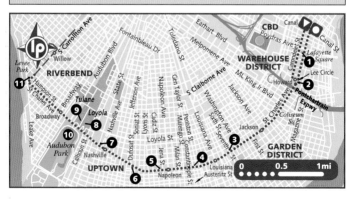

Magazine St

With six miles (10km) of shopping, Magazine St is best explored by public bus ($5 all-day pass). Catch the bus going uptown at Canal and Magazine Sts. At Sophie Wright Place ❶ in the Lower Garden District, hop off the bus to cruise the three-block strip of funky artists' studios, including Lionel Milton ❷ and Simon of New Orleans Gallery ❸, or the quirky rock shop of Southern Fossil & Mineral Exchange ❹. Pick up the bus at Jackson Ave to skip the ensuing multiblock residential area. Get off at Washington Ave ❺ to explore another small cluster of shops, such as Anton Haardt ❻, a Southern folk art gallery, or the sterling silver dealers of As You Like It Silver Shop ❼. Alternatively, get off the bus at Louisiana Ave ❽ to visit the street's largest collection of antique stores. Lilette ❾, at Antonine St, is a fashionable lunch stop, and Jean Bragg Antiques ❿ is a premier Southern art and antique dealer. Hop on the bus at Napoleon Ave to speed to the final cluster of shops starting at Jefferson Ave ⓫, where Beaucoup Books ⓬ and St Joe's Bar ⓭ round out the shopping experience. Catch the bus going downtown to return.

SIGHTS & HIGHLIGHTS

Lionel Milton's Gallery (p. 63)
Simon of New Orleans Gallery (p. 64)
Southern Fossil & Mineral Exchange (p. 69)
Anton Haardt Gallery (p. 61)
As You Like It Silver Shop (p. 61)
Lilette (p. 83)
Jean Bragg Antiques (p. 59)
Beaucoup Books (p. 67)
St Joe's Bar (p. 92)

distance 6 miles (10km)   **duration** 3hrs
▶ **start** 🚌 11 Magazine at Canal & Magazine Sts
● **end** 🚌 11 Magazine at Magazine St & Jefferson Ave

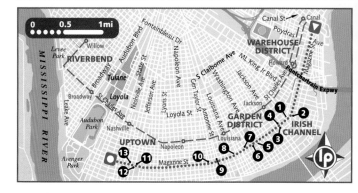

EXCURSIONS
River Road Plantations   (1, B8)

Preserved antebellum sugar plantations set along the curving course of the Mississippi River: doesn't it sound tranquil and romantic? *Au contraire* – the Mississippi is a serious laborer, not yet retired into tourism, and the disturbingly industrial petrochemical factories claim as much landscape as the fields of shaggy sugar cane or the few remaining historic homes. And forget about a view of the river itself – from the series of highways collectively referred to as the 'River Road,' you'll get a good look at the levee, a 15ft to 24ft tall grassy embankment.

Still interested? Then let's start plantation boot camp (the average person can take in two, maybe three, plantations before the tour guide's spiel about the clever 19th-century flycatcher becomes tiresome). Don't miss the 1805 **Laura Plantation**, a well-preserved West Indies–style building with impeccable family history and interesting descriptions of Creole customs. As a counterpoint, visit one (or two) of the American plantations. **Nottoway** (1849-59) is probably the best mix of history and architectural detail, but it is also the farthest from New Orleans. **Oak Alley** has its irresistible avenue of

INFORMATION

12-60 miles (19-97km) north-west of New Orleans

✉ Destrehan Plantation (13034 Hwy 48; ☎ 985-764-9315); San Francisco Plantation (2646 Hwy 44; ☎ 985-535-2341); Laura Plantation (2247 Hwy 18; ☎ 225-265-7690); Oak Alley (3645 Hwy 18; ☎ 225-265-2151); Nottoway Plantation (30970 Hwy 1; ☎ 225-545-2730)

ⓘ tickets purchased on-site

🕘 9am-5pm

💲 $10/5

✗ B&C Cajun Restaurant & Seafood Market (2155 Hwy 18, near Laura Plantation; ☎ 225-265-8356)

live oaks, but the tour is too much like watching *Gone with the Wind.* The Gothic steamboat-era **San Francisco Plantation** is as outrageous as the city with which it shares a name, although it is owned by its neighbor, Marathon Oil. **Destrehan Plantation** (1787) is spitting distance from New Orleans and historically interesting, but it was looted of most of its architectural finery and isn't as stunning as Nottoway or Oak Alley.

Be gone with the wind at Oak Alley

Barataria Preserve & Lafitte   (1, C9)

Plunge headlong into the prehistoric beauty of Louisiana's swamps at this national historic park, south of New Orleans. As you wind through the boardwalk paths, pulsating noises of invisible insects begin to mirror your internal biorhythms. Shallow water covered with a false carpet of duckweed mysteriously ripples with the morning commute of well-hidden creatures. The strengthening sun barely penetrates the thick canopy, and cypress knees jut out of the muck like rotten teeth; fan-like palmetos stand frozen when strangers approach. Only the mosquitoes and flies serve as swamp ambassadors. Through these lost water courses Jean Lafitte and his gang of pirates smuggled contraband from the Caribbean to New Orleans. No one dared venture too deep to apprehend him.

INFORMATION

20 miles (32km) south of New Orleans

- e www.nps.gov/jela/Barataria%20Preserve.htm
- i National Park Service Visitors Center (Hwy 3134; ☎ 504-589-2330); Jean Lafitte Tourist Office (Hwy 45; ☎ 800-689-3525)
- ☉ 9am-5pm
- $ free
- ✕ Voleo's Seafood (Hwy 45 & Nunez St; ☎ 689-3889; closed Sunday)

During the eight miles (13km) of hiking trails or nine miles (14km) of canoe routes, you will pass intimately close to sleeping alligators masquerading as gnarled logs, stoic fishing egrets and sunbathing turtles – the bigger the splash, the bigger the 'gator. Just outside the park, Jean Lafitte Inn (☎ 504-689-3271) rents canoes ($25) for self-guided tours through the preserve.

After a visit to the park, and for the sake of a ramble, take Hwy 45 south to the fishing villages of Jean Lafitte and Lafitte. There isn't much there, although travelling the ever-narrowing road to the very end, where the Intracoastal Hwy takes over, provides a good peek into the watery side of southern Louisiana. Perhaps the town's main attraction is Higgins Seafood market (☎ 689-3577), which sells pints of raw oysters fresh off the boat.

An alligator's view of Barataria Preserve

Cajun Country: St Martinville, Breaux Bridge & Lafayette (1, B5)

In 1755 French settlers living in Acadia, present-day Nova Scotia, were expelled by the new British overseers. What ensued is memorialized in the people's history as Le Grande Dérangement, when Acadian families were uprooted and wandered the US and Europe in exile. In 1785, seven boatloads of refugees arrived in Louisiana and made their way to the uninhabited swamps and prairies. More Acadians followed, eventually establishing a new homeland and a modified identity: Cajun.

On the banks of the Bayou Teche, two legendary Acadian lovers were said to have been briefly reunited under the boughs of the majestic **Evangeline Oak** in St Martinville; Longfellow's 1847 epic poem *Evangeline* was inspired by the bittersweet tale, and French is still spoken in this charming town. **St Martinville Cultural Heritage Center** recounts the histories of brothers in exile: the Acadians and Africans of southern Louisiana.

Lafayette, the self-crowned capital of Cajun Country, offers more cultural attractions. A healthy education on Acadiana can be found at the folklife museum of **Vermilionville** and the National Parks Service's **Acadian Cultural Center**. And a survey of the nightlife can be found in the city's many zydeco clubs.

If you're too beat to make it back to New Orleans, lay down beside the mythic waters of Bayou Teche in nearby Breaux Bridge. Overlooking the swift current, **Bayou Cabins**, which started out as a modest boudin and cracklin shop, has nine rustic cabins salvaged from Cajun homesteads. If the next morning is Saturday, your wanderlust might lead you to **Fred's Lounge** (p. 53) in Mamou.

Cajun Country: Mamou & Eunice   (1, A4)

It's 9am on a Saturday. Although the day is just warming up, **Fred's Lounge** in tiny Mamou is already packed and steamy. A four-piece Cajun band occupies the center of the bar, around which waltzing middle-aged couples expertly dodge spectators. Workaday guys and dolls guzzle Budweiser breakfasts, and Tante Sue, proprietor and bouncer, meets and greets the crowd between swigs of Hot Damn cinnamon schnapps. Fred's used to be a quiet bar in a quiet town, operated by its eponymous owner, Tante Sue's husband. When Fred died, Tante Sue only had time to open the place on Saturdays, even though the local bands were all booked at night. So she invited Wayne Thibodaux and Cajun Fever to play during the irregular hours of 9am to 1pm – the morning party has been a hit, drawing people from countless miles and countless countries away. The show is broadcast on KVPI 92.5FM.

In neighboring Eunice, the **Liberty Theater** presents Cajun music and dancing in a more wholesome setting. This 1920s-era theater stages 'Rendez-vous des Cajuns' on Saturday evenings, a live radio show sponsored by the National Park Service. Next door to the theater, the **Prairie Acadian Cultural Center** gives a cursory introduction to the Cajun culture in southwestern Louisiana.

INFORMATION

160 miles (258km) west of New Orleans

- ✉ Fred's Lounge (420 Sixth St; ☎ 3337-468-5411); Liberty Theater (S Second St & Park Ave; ☎ 337-457-8490); Prairie Acadian Cultural Center (Third St & Park Ave; ☎ 337-457-8490)
- ⓘ Eunice Chamber of Commerce (200 S Duson St; ☎ 337-457-2565); Evangeline Tourism Commission (704 N Soileau St, Ville Platte; ☎ 337-363-8687)
- ⊙ Fred's Lounge Sat 9am-1pm; Liberty Theater Sat 6-8pm; Cultural Center 9am-5pm
- $ free admission at Fred's and Cultural Center; Liberty Theater $5
- ✗ Mama's Fried Chicken (1640 W Laurel/Hwy 190; ☎ 337-457-9978)

Jerry Alexander

Bugging out at the Liberty Theater

ORGANIZED TOURS

African American Heritage Tours
This 3hr citywide tour covers the city's African-American heritage. There are also plantation tours and all-day Cajun village tours with zydeco music demonstrations. Reservations required.
☎ 288-3478 Ⓢ $45/75/85 city/Cajun village/plantation tour

Antoine's Restaurant
Join guide Carl Lezak on a tour of the 15 individually decorated private dining rooms at Antoine's restaurant (opened in 1840).
☎ 944-5498 ⏰ by appointment Ⓢ $10 per person (3 or more)

Captain Phil Robichaux
TV host Phil Robichaux runs 8hr Gulf Coast fishing tours from Lafitte Harbor Marina. Todd and Allen, his two most experienced guides, 'think like redfish.' The marina also rents waterfront cabins
(☎ 689-2013).
✉ 4775 Jean Lafitte Blvd ☎ 689-2006
Ⓢ $450 for 4 people

Carriage Tours
Guides offering mule-drawn carriage rides through the French Quarter, although certified by the city, indulge in requisite Big Easy embellishment. Carriages depart from Jackson Square, day and night until midnight.
Ⓢ $50 for up to 4 people

Chacahoula Swamp Tours
A true Cajun, Jerry Dupre leads 2hr intimate tours into Bayou Segnette aboard a 12-person shrimp boat, pointing out armadillo diggings and native plants and coaxing alligators to the boat.
✉ 422 Louisiana St, Westwego ☎ 436-2640 Ⓢ $25 per person plus $13 hotel pick-up

French Quarter Walking Tours
Friends of the Cabildo give 2hr tours of French Quarter architecture and history – with a dose of hard fiction – including free admission to two historic museums. Although no reservations are needed, arrive 10mins before departure.
✉ 523 St Ann St
☎ 523-3939 ⏰ Mon 1:30pm, Tues-Sun 10am & 1:30pm Ⓢ $10

Gay Heritage Tour
Robert Batson leads groups through the French Quarter, dispensing historical and humorous stories of local characters, including Tennessee Williams. Tours depart from the Alternatives Shop.
✉ 909 Bourbon St
☎ 945-6789 ⏰ Wed & Sat 1pm Ⓢ $20 for 4 people or more

Heritage Literary Tour
More than 60 authors have lived and written in New Orleans, leaving behind oral histories conveyed to you on this tour by Dr Kenneth Holditch, professor of literature at University of New Orleans.
✉ 732 Frenchmen St
☎ 949-9805 ⏰ by appointment Ⓢ $20

Historic New Orleans Walking Tours
The 2hr cemetery/voodoo tours visit St Louis Cemetery No 1 and the Voodoo Spiritual Temple. There are also walking tours of the Garden District and the French Quarter. Call for hours and tour departure location.
☎ 947-2120 Ⓢ $15

The pace in New Orleans is even slower by carriage

Le Monde Créole

Laura Locoul grew up on a Mississippi River sugar plantation. Thanks to her detailed diary, much is known about her life and the times. This 2½hr tour explores the French Quarter sites of her diary; reservations required. Tours are also given in French.
✉ **624 Royal St**
☎ **568-1801** ⊙ **Mon-Sat 10:30am & 1:30pm, Sun 10am & 1:30pm**
⑤ **$18**

Mr Denny's Voyageur Swamp Tour

With an uncanny resemblance to Dennis Hopper, Mr Denny leads 2hr, 8-mile (13km) canoe trips through Honey Island Swamp, gliding right up to sunbathing alligators and shimmying into moss-canopied slews. It's a welcome alternative to diesel-powered pontoon tours.
✉ **55344 Hwy 90 E, Slidell** ☎ **985-643-4839** ⑤ **$20/12 per adult/child plus $20 hotel pick-up**

Steamboat Natchez Cruise

The *Natchez* plies the Mississippi River – 2hr daytime cruises (with or without lunch) enjoy an onboard calliope organist, while 2hr evening cruises (with or without dinner) are serenaded by a Dixieland jazz band.
✉ **Toulouse St wharf, across from Jackson Sq**
☎ **586-8777**
⊙ **11:30am, 2:30pm & 6pm** ⑤ **$17 daytime cruise, $28 evening jazz cruise without meal**

Olivier Cirendini

Watch out for sneaky alligators in the bayou

Kickbacks and Marshmallows

Although they seem benign, the wildly popular swamp tours are big business, unscrupulously growing bigger. Sources say that the high-profile tour companies give out generous kickbacks to hotel concierges in return for referrals. The frequent sightings of the same company's brochure might not be coincidence; New Orleans makes a sport out of corruption.

Now, the alligators don't accept cash, but they get a little lagniappe from the tour companies as well. Most companies use flat-bottomed pontoons with outboard motors and a loudspeaker to project the guide's voice – it's quite a ruckus which scares away the star wildlife attractions. To satisfy the perfunctory 'gator-spotting, some tour companies feed the animals anything from chicken parts to marshmallows. This ranks a big 'zero' on the pro-environment meter, but the practice is so widespread, and the revenue so lucrative, that everyone turns a blind eye.

shopping

Once a booming port city, New Orleans was the destination for more European luxury goods in the mid-19th century than any other city in the USA. Swollen ships full of fine linens and haute furniture unloaded at the city's feet. Today, many survivors from that period are still sold on the very same streets where they started their American careers.

As New Orleans' industry segued from shipping to tourism, a new regime stepped in. From the ubiquitous Mardi Gras beads and feather boas to the shellacked alligator heads and voodoo dolls, all of New Orleans' unique customs have been packaged into cheap, Asian-made souvenirs eager to ride home in your suitcase.

Not nearly as well publicized is the city's vibrant arts community, flourishing in Julia St's formal galleries, makeshift stands on Jackson Square and empty lots in the Bywater. New artist immigrants from New York and San Francisco, out-priced in those cities' rental markets, have added even more creative juice and modernity to the scene. Stunning photographs, bold paintings and colorful glass pieces all rely on the spirit and flora of New Orleans for creative inspiration.

Shopping Areas

Refined **Royal St** has been a shopping venue since the mid-19th century. Creole families maintained their Frenchness through acquisitions of the latest rococo or Louis XV revival styles. The air of sophistication is still present today thanks to the street's architectural beauty and the numerous galleries and antique dealers centered on the blocks between Iberville and St Ann Sts. During business hours, portions of Royal St are closed to automobile traffic, further heightening the European feel.

The **French Market** (p. 22) and almost the entire length of **Decatur St** deal primarily to the tourist crowd in stereotypical New Orleans souvenirs, and the bustle and enthusiasm of the crowds can be infectious.

Magazine St runs roughly parallel to the river from Canal St to Audubon Park, passing through the Garden Districts and Uptown. At major avenues separating the different neighborhoods, clusters of shops reflect the tastes and attitudes of the nearby residents. As Magazine St is not a good candidate for a stroll, the handy **walking/bus tour** (p. 49) can help you form a shopping plan.

Opening Hours

Most shops in the French Quarter keep daily hours roughly between 10am and 5pm and abbreviated times on Sunday. However, New Orleans doesn't pay much mind to time, and shops that should be open aren't, without warning or notice. Outside the Quarter, shops typically close on Sunday and keep weekday hours with an abbreviated schedule on Saturday. Magazine St is dead on Sunday and quite erratic on other days. The Julia St galleries are closed Monday and Sunday.

DEPARTMENT STORES & SHOPPING CENTERS

Jackson Brewery
(6, H6) Formerly home to the failed Jax Brewery, this busy mall has 50 shops catering to gift and souvenir shoppers. A 3rd floor minimuseum documents the history of Jax beer, which was made by one of the largest independent breweries in the South.
✉ **600 Decatur St**
☎ **566-7245** ⏲ **Mon-Sat 11am-5:30pm, Sun noon-5pm**

New Orleans Shopping Centre
(5, E4) Lord & Taylor, Victoria's Secret and the Gap occupy this shopping center, next to the Superdome.
✉ **1400 Poydras Ave**
☎ **568-0000** 🚕 **cab or drive** ⏲ **Mon-Sat 10am-8pm, Sun noon-6pm**

Riverwalk Mall
(5, F10) With a stunning view of the Mississippi, this multistoried mall provides an easy, air-conditioned stroll for nearby convention-center escapees.

Sales Tax
Sales tax in New Orleans is 9%. International visitors can receive refunds on sales taxes (up to 10%) from more than 1000 Louisiana Tax Free Shopping (LTFS) stores. Look for the 'Tax Free' sign in store windows. Foreign visitors must show participating LTFS merchants a valid passport (Canadians may show a birth certificate or driving license) to receive a tax refund voucher. A complete listing of LTFS merchants is included in the *New Orleans Visitor Guide*, available free from the New Orleans Tourist and Convention Bureau (☎ 566-5005).

The Shops at Canal Place

Abercrombie & Fitch, Banana Republic and Sharper Image are a few of the many shopping options. It is also a good destination for a Riverfront streetcar ride.
✉ **1 Poydras Ave**
☎ **522-1555**
🚋 **Riverfront**
⏲ **Mon-Sat 10am-9pm, Sun 11am-7pm**

The Shops at Canal Place (6, K5)
This upscale mall houses Saks Fifth Avenue and Gucci, along with Williams-Sonoma and a multiplex showing mainstream and independent movies.
✉ **333 Canal St**
☎ **522-9200**
⏲ **Mon-Sat 10am-7pm, Sun noon-6pm**

Spend money like crazy at Riverwalk Mall

FASHION & JEWELRY

Funky Monkey
(3, G12) Didn't you want to be Wonder Woman last year for Halloween? Now is your chance. This used-clothing store sells our heroine's skimpy little outfit, as well as funky footwear and vintage clothes.

✉ **3127 Magazine St**
☎ **899-5587** 🚌 **11**
Magazine at Eighth St
🕐 **Mon-Sat 11am-6pm, Sun noon-5pm**

House of Lounge
(3, F14) A homegrown version of Victoria's Secret, House of Lounge gives boudoir fashion an injection of retro glamour. Ladies' dainties, men's smoking jackets and feathered slippers would be perfect for lounging around the house, sipping martinis and planning the steamer trip to Europe.

✉ **2044 Magazine St**
☎ **671-8300** 🚌 **11**
Magazine at Sophie Wright Place 🕐 **Mon-Sat 10am-6pm, Sun noon-5pm**

Il Negozio (3, H11)
Annoyed by those closet-sized boutiques with a selection of three dresses all in size zero? This stylish store actually has an assortment

Funky Monkey's shoes

of dresses, skirts, pants and blouses. What's more, it's in a charming old house with big picture windows and a real fitting room.

✉ **3607 Magazine St**
☎ **269-0130** 🚌 **11**
Magazine at Foucher St
🕐 **Tues-Sat 10am-5pm**

kun flam a (6, J5)
Even New Yorkers would be impressed by the selection of nightclub chic at this French Quarter boutique.

✉ **531 Iberville St**
☎ **586-1606**
🕐 **Mon-Fri 10am-5pm**

Meyer the Hatter
(5, D7) Since 1894, Meyer the Hatter has been selling fashions for the head. First, Stetson was all the rage, followed by Borsalino and now Dobbs and Kangol. Within the past few years Meyer has gone coed with a small selection of ladies' hats. Stop in for a tour of chapeau chic.

✉ **120 St Charles Ave**
☎ **525-1048** 🕐 **Mon-Sat 10am-5:45pm**

Mignon Faget (3, H10)
Newcomb-alumna Mignon Faget creates contemporary jewelry influenced by Louisiana flora and architecture. Medallion earrings, twig bracelets, tulip pendants and fleur-de-lis rings have won the artist international attention.

✉ **3801 Magazine St**
☎ **891-2005** 🚌 **11**
Magazine at General Taylor St 🕐 **Mon-Sat 10am-6pm**

Molly McNamara Designs (3, F14)
Pendants mimicking above-ground tombs or earrings evoking the curve of an oyster shell. Local artist Molly McNamara crafts New Orleans–inspired jewelry in this Lower Garden District shop.

✉ **2128 Magazine St**
☎ **566-1100** 🚌 **11**
Magazine at Sophie Wright Place 🕐 **Tues-Sat 10am-5pm**

Thrift City (4, J1)
Used clothes and bargains galore are packed like sardines into this beloved thrift store next to Mid-City Rock 'n' Bowl.

✉ **4125 S Carrollton Ave** 🚕 **cab or drive**
🕐 **Mon-Sat 10am-5pm, Sun noon-5pm**

Town & Country
(3, D14) Society maids and maidens come here for classic-style wedding dresses and ball gowns.

✉ **1512 St Charles Ave**
☎ **523-7027** 🚋 **St Charles at MLK Blvd**
🕐 **Mon-Sat 10am-6pm**

Trashy Diva (6, G6)
More than trashy, this Royal St boutique specializes in 1920s nightclub wear. Steel-boned corsets, classic-style chokers and real feather boas are at least fun to play dress-up with.

✉ **829 Chartres St**
☎ **581-4555**
🕐 **noon-6pm**

Victoria's Designer Shoes (6, H5)
Commonsense shoes are just too commonplace for this designer shoe store. Its straps and heels, sequins and stilettos grace the feet with sex appeal.

✉ **532 Chartres**
☎ **568-9990**
🕐 **10am-6pm**

ANTIQUES & INTERESTING JUNK

Antiques & Things
(3, G13) Vintage lamps, tables, dishes and rugs simulate the early '60s in all their thin-tie, organ-jazz glory. Faux furs and Jackie O hats can complete the foray into make-believe.
✉ **2855 Magazine St**
☎ **897-9466** 🚌 **11 Magazine St at Washington Ave**
🕐 **Mon-Sat 10am-5pm, Sun noon-5pm**

Architectural Salvage
(3, J10) Stone, metal and wooden orphans can be adopted at this quality junkyard. Jilted claws from old bathtubs, remnants of iron fences and termite-gnawed Victorian woodwork can be refashioned into bookends, headboards or wall art.
✉ **3965 Tchoupitoulas St** ☎ **891-6080** 🚌 **10 Tchoupitoulas at General Taylor St**
🕐 **Mon-Sat 10am-5pm**

The Garage (6, F7)
Follow Decatur St almost to the end toward Esplanade. Here the locals have elbowed out the tacky bead shops so popular elsewhere along this strip. At this grungy thrift shop, when the door is opened – the garage door, that is – you'll find lots of long-lost treasures, from well-worn camouflage to '50s bric-a-brac.
✉ **1234 Decatur St**
🕐 **Mon-Fri noon-4pm**

Jean Bragg Antiques
(3, H10) Even a traveler with only a vague interest in Southern art could benefit from a visit to Jean Bragg, the city's premier collection of work by trained regional artists. Keep an eye out for the realistic landscapes by painter Knute Heldner, the bulbous pots of George Ohr, and Arts and Crafts pottery from New Orleans' Newcomb school. Sadly, the snooty staff fails to extend the city's signature friendliness.
✉ **3901 Magazine St**
☎ **895-7375** 🚌 **11 Magazine at General Taylor** 🕐 **Mon-Sat 10am-5pm**

Jon Antiques (3, H8)
This direct importer has a large selection of mostly 18th- and 19th-century antiques from England. The store's collection of antique wooden boxes, including decanters, trunks and lap desks, is the real hallmark.
✉ **4605 Magazine St**
☎ **899-4482** 🚌 **11 Magazine at Cadiz St**
🕐 **Mon-Sat 10am-5pm**

Keil's Antiques (6, H4)
Keil's has three floors of French and English antiques, including dining-room and bedroom suites, mirrors, mantels, dinner rings and chandeliers.
✉ **325 Royal St**
☎ **522-4552**
🕐 **Mon-Sat 9am-5pm**

Lucullus Culinary Antiques, Art & Objects (6, H6)
The owner of Lucullus and author of *The Epicurean Collector: Exploring the World of Culinary Antiques* is an advocate of using, not collecting, culinary antiques because of the civilizing effects of beauty. Follow his advice and add more ritual and elegance to your life with an antique café au lait bowl or an absinthe spoon for creating the evening's cocktail.
✉ **610 Chartres St**
☎ **528-9620** 🕐 **Mon-Sat 9:30am-5pm**

Antiques & Things – would you like some junk with that tea?

A Mallard by Any Other Name

In New Orleans' historic houses and antique stores, you will meet the work of Monsieur Prudent Mallard (Ma-**lard**). Mahogany half-tester (modified canopy), four-poster beds and mammoth armoires are a few of the surviving pieces that this French-born, New Orleans–based craftsman made for the upper-crust Creole families of the mid-19th century – or at least, that's how the story goes. Recent research into the business transactions of P Mallard suggests that he was a better importer than cabinetmaker. Nowhere in Mallard's records is evidence of the manufacturing operations required to create as many pieces as he is credited with. A revised history based on these findings theorizes that he got his hands dirty during custom refinishing or upholstering but had no direct role in making the furniture except as a commissioner. Is a Mallard by another name just as beautiful? Most certainly.

Moss Antiques (6, H4)
This fourth-generation dealer specializes in 19th-century chandeliers and antique jewelry, inkwells and cigar humidors; it is affiliated with Keil's Antiques.
⊠ 411 Royal St
☎ 522-3981
⏱ Mon-Sat 9am-5pm

MS Rau Antiques
(6, G5) The oldest of the Royal St antique stores, MS Rau has a large and varied collection of European and American antiques. The store's cut glass, rare furniture, porcelain objets d'art and Louisiana jewelry outpaces many museum collections.
⊠ 630 Royal St
☎ 523-5660 ⏱ Mon-Sat 9am-5:15pm

New Orleans Cypress Works (3, G12)
If it is made of wood and has survived a few centuries in New Orleans, then it is probably made of cypress, a Louisiana-native softwood. At this Garden District shop, antique cypress from demolished houses is reassembled into handsome tables, bedframes and armoires, using the old-fashioned joinery techniques.
⊠ 3110 Magazine St
☎ 891-0001 🚃 11 Magazine at Eighth St
⏱ Mon-Sat 11am-5:30pm

Ondalee (6, F7)
Retro kitchenware, old postcards and interesting knickknacks fill this French Quarter second-hand boutique in the gutter-punk zone of Decatur.
⊠ 1231 Decatur St
☎ 581-3252 ⏱ Thurs-Tues 11am-5pm

Soniat House Antique Galleries
(6, F7) French painted furniture, 18th- and 19th-century Italian pieces, light fixtures and mirrors of exquisite quality; if you think the antiques for sale in this gallery are stunning, then you should see the affiliated luxury inn.
⊠ 1139 Chartres St
☎ 522-0570 ⏱ Mon-Sat 9am-5pm, closed for lunch noon-1pm

If shopping for antiques proves too taxing you can take a nap at Soniat House

ARTS & CRAFTS

Anton Haardt Gallery (3, G13)
Self-taught artist Mose Tolliver is indirectly responsible for the museum-quality collection of this Garden District gallery. Tolliver, a resident of Montgomery, Alabama, used to hang his paintings on trees in his front yard. Future gallery owner Anton Haardt took an interest, and bought one, then another, until he had a small collection and later this small business.
✉ 2858 Magazine St
☎ 891-9080
🚌 11 Magazine at Washington Ave
🕒 Tues-Sat 11am-5pm

Ariodante (5, G7)
Traditional crafts of maskmaking, glassblowing and batik are given modern interpretations at this Julia St gallery, which features regional and New Orleans–themed artists.
✉ 535 Julia St
☎ 524-3233 🚋 St Charles at Julia St
🕒 Mon-Sat 11am-5pm

Arthur Roger Gallery
(5, G7) On the modern side, this gallery profiles a rotating exhibit of local and regional artists. Highlights have included Michael Willmon's surrealistic oil paintings of New Orleans' ghost-riddled cemeteries.
✉ 432 Julia St
☎ 522-1999 🚌 11 Magazine at Julia St
🕒 Tues-Sat 10am-5pm

As You Like It Silver Shop (3, G12)
Collectors of rare and unique hollowware and flatware will find a

Folk Art
Without much ado, New Orleans has become a repository for Southern folk art. Like the blues, folk art grew out of rural communities isolated from modern trends of art appreciation. Oftentimes the unskilled artists were putting their emotions to paper or found objects, unaware that their childlike renditions captured unifying Southern themes of religion, racism and family. The Ogden Museum of Southern Art (p. 34) is a good warm-up for exploring 'outsider' art, as is Madame John's Legacy (p, 37). Private dealers of folk art include Peligro! Folk Art Gallery (p. 63) and Anton Haardt Gallery (p. 61). You can also purchase folk art directly from the artists' studios, such as Dr Bob's Studio (p. 61) and the Simon of New Orleans Gallery (p. 64).

stunning array at this Magazine St shop. It also carries obsolete patterns by the set or the piece.
✉ 3033 Magazine St
☎ 897-6915 🚌 11 Magazine at Eighth St
🕒 Mon-Sat 10am-5pm

Berta's & Mina's Antiquities (3, H9)
Littered with canvases and reeking of oil paint, this Magazine St studio displays the work of Nilo Lanzas, who took up a paint brush at age 63 just after his wife's death. His work is modern naive, depicting alligators on shopping trips, rockabilly singers and religious pilgrims.
✉ 4138 Magazine St
☎ 895-6201 🚌 11 Magazine at Marengo St 🕒 10am-6pm

Bywater Art Market
Word about a place with cheap rent and disinterested neighbors usually spreads. An area may be a slum to some, but to others it's a 'bohemia.' In the

1920s the French Quarter held this title and attracted such greats as William Faulkner and Tennessee Williams. Now the Bywater modestly wears this distinction. Before time crowns the next Southern artists, you can browse the contestants at the Bywater Art Market, held on the third Saturday of every month.
✉ 3301 Chartres at Piety ☎ 944-7990
🚌 cab or drive
🕒 3rd Sat of every month 9am-3pm

Dr Bob's Studio (2, C9)
Bob Shaffer used to be a forest ranger, not an artist. In his spare time, he would carve animals out of wood for friends and family. One day he ran out of wood and the next day he was a painter. Now his brightly colored works of bayou creatures and the popular slogan 'Be Nice or Leave' have become New Orleans pop icons.
✉ 3000 Chartres St
☎ 945-2225 🕒 by appointment or chance

Art as a Storyteller

Local artist George Schmidt kindly answered a few questions about his work as an historical painter. He and his canvases can be viewed at his 626 Julia St gallery.

How does New Orleans serve as your historical muse? The dead live again in New Orleans and through painting they rise again. Everything we appreciate about New Orleans is culturally conservative; it is a city that is turned toward its past.

What is your favorite period of New Orleans history? I would pick the 1890s and the turn of the 19th century, when the last wave of European immigration occurred. People were still speaking German and Italian in the streets, and New Orleans was a Catholic city then.

Explain your aversion to the modern. I describe myself as an antimodernist. I was born in the wrong century. I tried to be a modernist but it makes me unhappy. And, in terms of painting, modern painters create signs and symbols; modern painting is like tourism, always promoting itself. It doesn't tell a story. I do narrative art. I hear a story and I paint the images that come to mind.

A Gallery for Fine Photography (6, H5)

The history of photography is cataloged at this French Quarter gallery of original prints. Rare Storyville scenes by EJ Bellocq and early shots of New Orleans from William Henry Jackson are worth investigating. The changing exhibits on the 2nd floor have featured such renowned artists as Marion Post Wolcott and George Zimbel.

✉ **241 Chartres St**
☎ **568-1313** ◷ **Mon-Sat 10am-6pm, Sun 11am-6pm**

George Schmidt Gallery (5, G6)

In this Julia St gallery, the city's past unfolds with lifelike characters and intriguing subplots. Mardi Gras, jazz musicians and famous parties, all dating from before 1950, have posed as the artist's imagined subjects.

✉ **626 Julia St** ☎ **592-0206** 🚋 **St Charles at Julia St** ◷ **Tues-Sat 12:30pm-4:30pm**

La Belle Galerie (6, J4)

Photographs of New Orleans' brass bands and acrylics of Preservation Hall make up a small portion of this gallery's huge selection of African-American art. Limited edition prints by national artists and Jazz Fest posters are also available.

✉ **309 Chartres St**
☎ **529-3080**
◷ **10am-7pm**

Lighthouse Glass (5, F7)

This unusual hands-on gallery actively encourages browsers to hold and admire local artists' work in handmade glass, including everyday jewelry.

✉ **743 Camp St**
☎ **529-4494**
🚋 **St Charles at Julia St** ◷ **Tues-Sat 12:30pm-6pm**

Lighthouse Glass – this gallery will light up your life

Lionel Milton's Gallery (3, E15)
An alumnus of the Ya/Ya youth program, Lionel Milton creates fresh pop scenes with graffiti fluidity and hip-hop attitude. His cartoonlike characters have been recruited for an animated TV series based in New Orleans.
✉ 1818 Magazine St
☎ 522-6966 🚌 11 Magazine at Sophie Wright Place ⏰ Tues-Sat 10am-5pm

New Orleans School of Glass Works & Printmaking Studio
(5, F7) Visitors can view artists at work in their printmaking, bookbinding and hot glass studios during nonsummer months. A small gallery sells pieces made by the artists.
✉ 727 Magazine St.
☎ 529-7277 🚌 11 Magazine St at Julia St ⏰ Mon-Sat 11am-5pm

Peligro! Folk Art Gallery (6, J5)
It is unusual to find an unpolished gallery in the French Quarter, but Peligro is a refreshing change. The gallery's specialty of Southern folk art is sold at prices real folks can afford.
✉ 305 Decatur St
☎ 581-1706 ⏰ Mon-Thurs 10am-6pm, Fri-Sat 10am-10pm, Sun noon-6pm

Photo Works (6, G6)
The shadow of an intricate cast-iron balcony, the acrobatic bend in the Mississippi River and the mad throng of people on Bourbon St are preserved in color and in black and white by veteran photographer Louis Sahuc.
✉ 839 Chartres St

Cover Art
Next time you beat a path to Bourbon St, take a good look at the sidewalk (or 'banquette' in local parlance) for a water meter cover. Notice the covers decorated with an Art Deco–style crescent moon and stars? These are designs from the Ford Meter Box Company of Wabash, Indiana, which first developed the technology for curbside metering. The design was so popular that people would steal the covers, leaving behind gaping holes and a very serious public-safety problem. In response, local artists applied the distinctive design to porcelain, glass and metal to create a safer and more portable souvenir. Studio Inferno (p. 64) prints the design on vibrantly colored glass about the size of a coaster. Lazybug (600 Royal St; 6, G5; ☎ 524-3649) sells a hand-painted ceramic reproduction by Robert Horan, and Lighthouse Glass (p. 62) has handy key chains.

☎ 593-9090 ⏰ Thurs-Mon 10am-5:30pm

Rhino Gallery (6, F6)
This nonprofit co-op features the work of Louisiana artists in a variety of decorative media. Wooden tomb boxes, Studio Inferno glass pieces and pottery line the shelves in a hassle-free, art-for-art's-sake zone.
✉ 927 Royal St
☎ 569-8191
⏰ Mon-Sat 10am-6pm, Sun 11am-6pm

Rodrigue Studio
(6, G6) Déjà vu will strike as you enter the gallery of George Rodrigue. Where have you seen that zombie-eyed blue dog before? Actually, where haven't you seen it? Rodrigue's signature subject, the Blue Dog, was a pop sensation at the close of the 20th century, appearing in Absolut vodka ads and the TV show *Friends*.
✉ 721 Royal St
☎ 581-4244
⏰ Mon-Sat 10am-6pm, Sun noon-5pm

Had enough of happy hour? Go highbrow at Stella Jones

Simon of New Orleans Gallery (3, F14)

Affable Simon Hardeveld paints signs – colorful signs with simple lettering advertising burgers or common expressions. The popular New Orleans slogan 'Be Nice or Leave' appears in bold colors on scrap plywood. His personal favorite is 'Shalom Y'all,' which he's painted over and over again for satisfied customers. Got a slogan on the tip of your tongue? He'll paint that for you, too.

✉ **2126 Magazine St**
☎ **561-0088** 🚌 **11 Magazine at Sophie Wright Place** ☉ **Thurs-Sat 10am-5pm**

Stella Jones Gallery (5, D7)

African-American, Caribbean and African art document the experience of the diaspora through high-quality paintings, sculptures and photography. Stop in while you are waiting for the St Charles streetcar.

✉ **201 St Charles Ave**
☎ **568-9050**
☉ **Mon-Fri 11am-6pm, Sat noon-5pm**

Studio Inferno (6, E11)

Colorful cast and blown glass pieces are produced in this Bywater studio, formerly a bottling factory. Visitors can view artists at work on the hot shop floor or just hang around feeling that they are part of a reviving art form.

✉ **3000 Royal St**
☎ **945-1878** 🚕 **cab or drive** ☉ **Mon-Fri 9am-5pm, Sat 10am-5pm**

A Studio on Desire (2, C9)

The poignant work of Christopher Porché West can occupy an afternoon of contemplation. He photographs people who, without a word, speak directly to the viewer, telling them about being a Mardi Gras Indian, leading a jazz march or cleaning the grave of a loved one.

✉ **917 Desire St**
☎ **947-3880** 🚕 **cab or drive** ☉ **by appointment or chance**

UP/Unique Products (3, F15)

Recycled tea-biscuit tins, empty detergent bottles and other found objects get reincarnated as artistic houzewares by the husband-and-wife team of Mark Kirk and Heather Macfarlane. Area restaurants frequently sport their Mardi Gras–bead light fixture, which looks like a colorful jellyfish.

✉ **2038 Magazine St**
☎ **529-2441** 🚌 **11 Magazine at Sophie Wright Place**
☉ **Mon-Sat 10am-5pm**

Visual Jazz Gallery (6, C9)

The work of Richard Thomas can be viewed at this gallery. Thomas created the mural of New Orleans music legends that greets incoming flights at the Louis Armstrong airport. His posters for Mardi Gras and Jazz Fest put an Andy Warhol-esque spin on New Orleans personalities.

✉ **2337 St Claude Ave**
☎ **949-9822**
🚕 **cab or drive**
☉ **by appointment**

Young Aspirations/Young Artists (Ya/Ya) (5, E5)

This nonprofit center directs the creative energies of inner-city youths into art professions and visual expression. It is structured like an apprentice guild, and students work with artist-teachers in after-school programs painting batik, furniture and canvas. Once their work is sellable, they make 50% to 80% of the piece's value. Swatch watches and the UN General Assembly have commissioned pieces, and Ya/Ya graduates have gone on to establish their own art careers in New Orleans.

✉ **601 Baronne St**
☎ **529-3306** 🚋 **St Charles at Lafayette St**
☉ **Mon-Fri 9am-5pm**

FOOD & DRINK

Bayou Country (6, H6)
The money might just march out of your pockets at this energetic food and gift shop. Hot sauces, Cajun spices, gift baskets and goofy souvenirs all want to join you back home.
✉ 3rd fl, Jackson Brewery Mall
◷ 10am-5pm

Central Grocery
(6, G7) The muffuletta's birthplace also sells imported goods from Italy, Creole filé powder for sprinkling on gumbo, and seasonings used by all the Louisiana cooks.
✉ 923 Decatur St
☎ 523-1620 ◷ Mon-Sat 8am-5:30pm, Sun 9am-5:30pm

Laura's Candies
(6, F6) Truffles, specialty chocolates and handmade candies are just the gift for a sweet-toothed someone. Laura's Mississippi mud pralines are made with caramel, pecans, and milk or dark chocolate. Are you sure you want to leave New Orleans?
✉ 938 Royal St
☎ 525-3880
◷ 10am-6pm

Martin Wine Cellar
(3, F10) A bit of a trek from St Charles Ave, this homage to wine rivals most urban grocery stores in size. To navigate the rows of common and rare wines and Champagnes, ask the staff for recommendations and even a couple of samples when nearing a decision. The cellar also hosts food tastings throughout the store.
✉ 3827 Baronne St

☎ 899-7411 🚕 cab or drive ◷ Mon-Sat 9am-7pm, Sun 10am-4pm

New Orleans School of Cooking (6, H5)
The general store of this cooking school has a good selection of useful products. Ellis Stansel's gourmet rice, Kevin's seasoning blend and Cajun Power sauce (a mixture of roasted red pepper and garlic) will do more than collect dust on your kitchen counter.
✉ 524 St Louis St
☎ 525-2665
◷ 9:15am-5pm

Southern Candy Makers (6, J5)
Generous samples allow you to choose just the right kind of praline for your post-visit savoring. Rhode Island–sized chunks of pecans, not skimpy pecan dust, appear in Southern's award-winning pralines. The store also has a selection of taffy and other candies.
✉ 334 Decatur St
☎ 523-5544
◷ 10am-5pm

Uncle Wilbur's Emporium (6, F7)
This Decatur St shop is one of many sellers of Café du Monde products, such as chicory coffee and beignet mix. The usual suspects of postcards, beads and plastic crawfish can be found among the store's other gift options.
✉ 1039 Decatur St
☎ 581-2914
◷ 9am-5pm

Vieux Carré Wine & Spirits (6, H5)
Don't let the pickled-looking guys out front deter you from wandering around this neighborhood wine shop. Top-shelf tequilas, Scotches and Champagnes will cure what ails you. An extensive selection of wines covers the globe, but some aficionados recommend going with popular varieties, as rarer vintages might suffer here from Louisiana's ungracious heat.
✉ 422 Chartres St
☎ 568-9463 ◷ Mon-Sat 10am-10pm, Sun 10am-7pm

Pig out at Laura's Candies

VOODOO & OCCULT

Esoterica Occult Goods (6, G7)

Burgeoning witches and goths can obtain all their sorcery needs here – from books and talismans to charms and herbs. The store also hosts a nightly witchcraft tour.

✉ 541 Dumaine St
☎ 581-7711
🕑 noon-10pm

Historic Voodoo Museum

(6, G6) Lost your keys or think your lover has developed a wandering eye? The gift shop of this museum sells candles and potions to bend fate and the future. At the 217 N Peters St shop, Friday night voodoo rituals are held for the public.

✉ 724 Dumaine St
☎ 523-7685
🕑 10am-8pm

Starling Magickal Books & Crafts (6, F6)

Specializing in witchcraft, voodoo and mythology, this used-bookstore also carries essential oils, artwork and jewelry.

✉ 1022 Royal St
☎ 595-6777 🕑 Thurs-Mon noon-7pm

Voodoo Spiritual Temple (6, F5)

Priestess Miriam does African bone readings and palm readings for open-minded seekers. Just across the street from Congo Square, where many early voodoo rituals were held, her small shop also sells the requisite voodoo objects and dolls.

✉ 828 N Rampart St
☎ 522-9627
🕑 10am-5pm

Zombie's House of Voodoo (6, G5)

Less crowded than its Bourbon St sister location, this store sells a variety of charms and gris gris, from stone arrowheads to correct a bad sense of direction, to the perennial favorite, love potion No 9. Zombie's also has a large selection of voodoo statues, including one of Marie Laveau. If you can bear the naked truth of the tarot cards, readings are more intimate here than on Jackson Square.

✉ 723 St Peter St
☎ 486-6366
🕑 10am-11:30pm

Charming Esoterica Occult

MARDI GRAS

Little Shop of Fantasy (6, H5)

These elaborate handmade masks are crafted out of papier mâché, leather or cloth and are encircled with feathers and jewels. Some evoke medieval European masking traditions, while others look exactly like Cher.

✉ 517 St Louis St
☎ 529-4243
🕑 Mon-Sat 11am-6pm, Sun 1-6pm

Royal Rags (6, G6)

With a picture or a good description, Laura Roe can turn your Mardi Gras whimsy into a custom-made costume. She also caters for large sizes.

✉ 627 Dumaine St
☎ 566-7247
🕑 call for hours

Uptown Costume & Dancewear (3, H9)

Looking for something suitably shocking for Halloween, Mardi Gras or your brother's wedding? Robot-zombies, Vegas Elvis and fat body suits are just some of the store's wacky costumes. Don't forget the face glitter or long eyelashes for Sunday dinner.

✉ 4326 Magazine St
☎ 895-7969 🚌 11 Magazine at Napoleon Ave 🕑 Mon-Fri 10am-6pm, Sat 10am-5pm

Zulu Social Aid & Pleasure Club (4, H4)

Posters and memorabilia of the Zulus, a famous African-American Mardi Gras krewe, are sold at the club's Mid-City office.

✉ 722 N Broad Ave
☎ 827-1661 🚖 cab or drive 🕑 Sat 10:30am-5:30pm

BOOKS

Arcadian Books (6, G5)
Peek behind those floor-to-ceiling stacks of books to find proprietor Russell Desmond, who speaks both French and English. Close to a decade ago, Lonely Planet characterized him as a cynical ambassador for New Orleans – not much has changed.
✉ **714 Orleans St**
☎ **523-4138** ◷ **Mon-Sat 10:30am-6pm, Sun noon-5pm**

Beaucoup Books
(3, H6) This Magazine St bookstore draws many contemporary authors for readings, and offers a wide selection of general-interest and regional titles; it also hosts children's events.
✉ **5414 Magazine St**
☎ **895-2663** 🚌 **11 Magazine at Jefferson Ave** ◷ **Mon-Sat 10am-6pm, Sun noon-5pm**

Beckham's Book Store (6, J5)
Rare and second-hand books line the walls of this bibliophile's haunt. Classical records, piano rolls and old prints complete the collection.
✉ **228 Decatur St**
☎ **522-9875**
◷ **10am-6pm**

Maple Street Children's Book Shop (p.69)

Bookworm Choices

Want to become a dime-store historian? Peruse some of these titles on your next bookstore visit. *Old New Orleans* by Stanley Clisby Arthur details French Quarter architecture and history. *The Free People of Color of New Orleans* by Mary Gehman gives a brief overview of black Creole culture. *Frenchmen, Desire, Good Children & Other Streets of New Orleans* by cartoonist John Churchill Chase explores the city's history through its unusual street names.

Literary New Orleans edited by Richard S Kennedy is a series of essays on famous New Orleans writers and their relationship with the city.

Mardi Gras Indian by Michael P Smith peers inside this African-American Mardi Gras tradition.

Gumbo Ya Ya is a collection of Louisiana stories gathered by the Federal Writers Program of the 1930s.

Robert Florence's *New Orleans Cemeteries: Life in the Cities of the Dead* is a beautifully illustrated odyssey through the city's unique culture of laying loved ones to rest.

Community Book Center (4, J4)
In Mid-City, this bookstore specializes in African-American titles ranging from modern social commentaries to histories of jazz and free people of color. Poetry and prose readings are also held here.
✉ **217 N Broad Ave**
☎ **822-2665** 🚕 **cab or drive** ◷ **Mon-Sat 10am-7pm**

Faulkner House
(6, G6) This bookstore (and former residence of William Faulkner) sells rare first editions of Southern writers. Less precious editions of past and present forces in Southern literature are carried as well; some new names to check out include John Gregory Brown, Tim Gautreaux and Jim Grisley.
✉ **624 Pirate's Alley**
☎ **524-2940**
◷ **10am-6pm**

Kaboom Books (6, E7)
Tucked away on the far-flung edge of the Quarter, this general-interest used-bookstore is easy to navigate and hard to leave; don't worry, no one here is in a rush.
✉ **901 Barracks St**
☎ **529-5780**
◷ **11am-6pm**

MUSIC

Jim Russell Records

(3, E15) This dusty Lower Garden District shop boasts over a million new and used LPs from Louisiana music to rock and hip-hop. The store's strength is in its 45s collection, and its weakness is its collectors' prices.

✉ 1837 Magazine St
☎ 522-2602 🚌 11 Magazine at Sophie Wright Place
🕐 Mon-Sat 10am-7pm, Sun 1-6pm

Louisiana Music Factory (6, J5)

From R&B to Dixieland, Louisiana Music Factory has one of the widest selections of regional music in the city. Listening stations for both CDs and vinyl allow you to test drive new and used products. The staff loves to talk shop, so have plenty of free time.

✉ 210 Decatur St
☎ 586-1094 🕐 Mon-Sat 10am-7pm, Sun 11am-7pm

Pick up some rare vinyl

SPECIALIST SHOPS

Aidan Gill For Men

(3, F15) This lower Magazine shop has recreated all the romantic notions of the old-style barbershop when the shaves were close, the snifters strong and the haircuts precise. Supplies for the gentleman's toilet are also sold.

✉ 2026 Magazine St
☎ 587-9090 🚌 11 Magazine at Sophie Wright Place 🕐 Tues-Fri 10am-6pm, Sat 9am-5pm

Anne Rice Collection

(3, F12) Louis, Armand, Lestat and other characters from Anne Rice's novels have gone commercial with a line of dolls and keepsakes. Serious Rice-heads should stop here to view the wedding dress that she wore for her mock funeral.

✉ 2nd fl, 2727 Prytania St mall
☎ 899-5996 🚃 St Charles at Washington Ave 🕐 Mon-Sat 10am-6pm, Sun 11am-4pm

Civil War Store (6, J5)

This closet-sized store specializes in Confederate memorabilia from rifles and pistols to bonds and stamps. It is also developing a minor in WWII artifacts.

✉ 212 Chartres St
☎ 522-3328
🕐 Mon-Sat 10:30am-5:30pm

Hové Parfumeur

(6, G6) Grassy vetivert, bittersweet orange blossoms, spicy ginger – New Orleans' exotic flora has graciously lent its scents to Hové's house-made perfumes for over 70 years. A brief sniffing visit will leave your head swirling with images of the Vieux Carré's magnificent past. Tom Robbins was clearly impressed; he loosely based scenes from his novel *Jitterbug Perfume* on this very store.

✉ 824 Royal St
☎ 525-7827
🕐 Mon-Sat 10am-5pm

James H Cohen & Sons (6, H5)

Looking to replace your mother-of-pearl opera glasses? Or complete your collection of Confederate coins? For the serious collector or the serious gawker, this family-owned store is a quirky but informative browse.

✉ 437 Royal St
☎ 522-3305
🕐 9:30am-5:30pm

Three Dog Bakery

(6, G6) Dogs are not only humanity's best friends, they are connoisseurs of better baked goods. Thanks to Three Dog Bakery, sawdust doggie treats can be foisted off on the toddler. Modern dogs want Scottie biscotti, Snickerpoodles or other punning, all-natural treats. Sorry Rufus, no garbage-flavored biscuits.

✉ 827 Royal St
☎ 525-2253 🕐 Wed-Sat 11am-6pm

FOR CHILDREN

Big Life Toys (3, H6)
Sanrio's Hello Kitty, Bozart designs and tin toys will keep those retro-loving gen-xers forever young. Real kids with urban sensibilities will also be amused.
✉ **5430 Magazine St**
☎ **899-8697** 🚌 **11 Magazine at Jefferson Ave** ⏲ **Mon-Sat 1am-6pm, Sun 11am-5pm**

Capelle Inc Little Toy Shop (6, G7)
Little kids literally sprint to this toy shop of metal soldiers, die-cast cars and trucks, dolls and books. Parents aren't far behind with the credit card.
✉ **900 Decatur St**
☎ **522-6588**
⏲ **9am-7pm**

Idea Factory (6, G6)
Hand-carved wooden toys and machines, puzzle boxes and wall hangings make lifelong gifts for children and lovely coffee-table pieces for grown-ups.
✉ **838 Chartres St**
☎ **524-5195** ⏲ **Mon-Sat 10am-6pm, Sun 10am-5pm**

Maple Street Children's Book Shop (3, C3) For young booklovers, this Uptown shop specializes in children's books, from Mardi Gras stories to Cajun folk tales, and hosts afternoon story time and book signing parties.
✉ **7529 Maple St**
☎ **861-2105** 🚕 **cab or drive** ⏲ **10am-6pm**

Capelle Inc Little Toy Shop

Pippen Lane (3, G12)
For parents who want baby dolls for children, Pippen Lane offers a beautiful selection of imported clothing too nice for the average tyke.
✉ **2929 Magazine St**
☎ **269-1006** 🚌 **11 Magazine at Seventh St** ⏲ **Mon-Fri 10am-6pm, Sat 10am-5pm**

Southern Fossil & Mineral Exchange (3, F14) Part museum, part freak show, the Exchange is chock full of taxidermy, including a gaping stuffed alligator, and display cases of skulls. If you've failed with the rabbit's foot, an alligator key chain might bring some bayou luck.
✉ **2045 Magazine St**
☎ **523-5525** 🚌 **11 Magazine at Sophie Wright Place** ⏲ **Sat noon-4pm**

Join in the freak show at Southern Fossil & Mineral Exchange

places to eat

E ating in New Orleans is a serious pursuit, as fervently followed as college football and more hotly debated than politics or religion. Finding the best gumbo, po'boy, rising chef or old-line restaurant consumes countless hours of selfless devotion, and an equal amount of time discussing, or arguing, one's findings.

New Orleans' ensemble of restaurants can be roughly divided into three categories: old-line, nouvelle and neighborhood. Leading the parade are the old-line restaurants, such as Galatoire's, Antoine's and Brennan's. These are family owned, fine-dining establishments that were instrumental in the evolution of Creole cuisine. Time-honored traditions of service and decorum far eclipse the more modern concept of a chef. Recipes are meticulously re-created, without deviation, as they were first served, in some cases, more than 100 years ago. Within

Meal Costs

The pricing symbols used in this chapter indicate the cost for 1 person of a 2-course meal, excluding drinks.

$	under $15
$$	$16-25
$$$	$26-50
$$$$	over $50

these understated dining halls reeking of history, well-placed (and well-dressed) New Orleans families arrive on a Friday afternoon for lunch and stay until dinner. Their server, who they might have inherited along with grandmother's house, has their cocktail and first course ready before they are seated at a table. A watered-down version of this privileged world is offered to tourists with varying degrees of diplomacy; to ensure a smooth ride, place yourself in the able hands of the server, the gatekeeper to an enjoyable experience, and dress appropriately.

More egalitarian and familiar are the nouvelle-cuisine restaurants, which rival those of New York and San Francisco. These chef-driven eateries offer seasonal menus blooming with unique combinations of international and Creole elements, a fine wine list and stylish dining rooms. Restaurant spectators crafted the term 'Louisiana contemporary' to define the styles of such restaurants as Bayona, Emeril's, K-Paul's and Peristyle. The only passports required for entry are reservations and business attire.

The neighborhood joints are where New Orleans can truly be savored. This is no frills, no reservations, no dress code, good eating. The ambience is supplied solely by the eccentric regulars or minor celebrity owners, who have run the place for as long as anyone can remember. Po'boys, gumbos, soups and various fried concoctions simplify the ingredients but complicate the ordering decision. (These restaurants are classified in this chapter as 'New Orleans'.)

On the practical side, make reservations whenever possible and as far in advance as possible. Restaurants without reservation policies are typically swamped, and an hour or more wait is common. Many restaurants close during the summer months, so call ahead. And remember to save room for dessert.

FRENCH QUARTER, FAUBOURG MARIGNY & BYWATER

Acme Oyster House (6, J4) $

Seafood

These bad mother-shuckers might crack open 4000 to 5000 oysters a night. All you have to do is sidle up to the bar, order a dozen and knock 'em back. The men's record is 41 dozen, the women's a meager 16. Are you up for the challenge?

✉ 724 Iberville St
☎ 835-6410 ⏰ Mon-Sat 11am-10pm, Sun noon-7pm ♿

Antoine's (6, H5) $$$

Creole

In some cities a restaurant dating from 1840 and run by a fifth-generation family would be a death curse, but in New Orleans it is paramount to nobility. While the dishes may disappoint modern palates, Antoine's offers a remarkable time capsule of 19th-century tastes. Place yourself in the hands of the waiter for navigating the French menu. Jackets required; reservations recommended.

✉ 713-717 St Louis St
☎ 581-4422
⏰ Mon-Sat 11:30am-2pm, 5:30-9:30pm

French Quarter Highlights
Forget where your friends told you to eat and head straight to **Bayona** (p. 71), for one of the best fine-dining experiences in New Orleans and easily the best meal of your life. On the scruffier side of the culinary spectrum, **Johnny's Po-Boys** (p. 75) is a great introduction to these signature sandwiches.

Central Grocery (p. 73) invented muffulettas, but **Luigi's** (p. 76) perfected the recipe; you might find yourself craving these Frisbee-shaped sandwiches on the flight home. **Acme Oyster House** (p. 71) is bushels of fun; try to get a seat at the oyster bar to watch the shuckers in action. If you can score a bar stool at **Port of Call** (p. 77) when locals have docked, you'll see New Orleans' drinking and eating culture in its purest form.

For classic Creole, don your suit jacket for an evening's worth of dining at **Galatoire's** (p. 75).

Arnaud's Restaurant (6, H4) $$$

Creole

For a little contrast, step off sweaty Bourbon St into Arnaud's elegant dining room (jacket required) to sample oysters Bienville – an original with shrimp, mushrooms, green onions and spices – and other Creole dishes. The Richelieu Room, where an acoustic jazz ensemble plays, is less formal (business casual).

✉ 813 Bienville St
☎ 523-5433
⏰ Mon-Fri 11:30am-2:30pm, 6-10pm, Sat 6-10:30pm, Sun 10am-3:30pm, 6-10pm

Bayona (6, H4) $$$

Louisiana Contemporary

Local ingredients get top billing in chef Susan Spicer's innovative and international dishes, such as grilled shrimp with black-bean cake and coriander sauce, or crabmeat and fried green tomatoes with caper-shallot vinaigrette. As an encore, try the delicious house-made ice cream or sorbet. The dining parlors, in a converted Creole cottage, are as charming as the food. Dinner reservations required; business casual.

✉ 430 Dauphine St
☎ 525-4455 ⏰ Mon-Fri 11:30am-2pm, Mon-Thurs & Sun 6-9:30pm, Fri-Sat 6-9pm **V**

Old-school Antoine's

Belle Forché (6, F8) $$

Creole

Catering to the young spenders of Frenchmen St, Belle Forché fuses Creole with an international body of flavors, with varying success. Its real strength is a late-night menu and a party ambience.

✉ **1407 Decatur St**
☎ **940-0722** ⏱ Tues-Thurs & Sun 5:30-10:30pm, Fri-Sun 11:30am-2:30pm, Fri-Sat 5:30pm-2:30am **V**

Brennan's New Orleans (6, H5) $$$

Creole

No shame to it, we've all nipped before noon and now's the chance to do it again. Brennan's famous breakfast/brunch makes the morning cocktail a first, second and...course. Ramos gin fizz and milk punch 'eye openers' help stimulate the appetite for eggs Hussarde or omelette Florentine. Reservations required; ask for the upstairs balcony.

✉ **417 Royal St**

Feeling wooden? Perk up with an eye opener at Brennan's

Light My Fire

Some parts of the country invent superconductors, electric light bulbs, or other useless crap, while New Orleans invents food. Bananas Foster, a classic American dessert, was born at Brennan's Restaurant in 1951. The pyromaniac chef sliced a few bananas, sauteed them in butter, brown sugar, cinnamon and liqueur, and then set the whole mess ablaze with some rum. Folks are suckers for fiery dishes.

☎ **525-9711** ⏱ 8am-2:30pm, 6-10pm

Bywater Bar-B-Que (2, C2) $

Southern/American

Diving deeper into the Bywater, you'll find this place inhabited by tattooed, bike-riding artists who scrape together enough to splurge on tasty pulled-pork sandwiches, spare ribs or fried catfish.

✉ **3162 Dauphine St**
☎ **944-4445** 🚌 **5 Marigny/Bywater at Louisa** ⏱ Mon-Fri 6am-10pm, Sat-Sun 11am-10pm ♿ **V**

Cafe Beignet (6, H5) $

Café/Breakfast

Not to be confused with Café du Monde, this quaint nook has a shaded patio and serves French-style omelettes as well as deli sandwiches.

✉ **334B Royal St**
☎ **522-6868**
⏱ 7am-5pm **V**

Café du Monde (6, G6) $

Café

You won't have to deliberate over a lengthy menu at this New Orleans classic. The choices are easy: beignets and café au lait. Beignets are square pieces of dough, deep fried and dusted with sugar. What a glorious morning.

✉ **800 Decatur St**
☎ **581-2914** ⏱ 24hrs

Café Negril (6, E8) $$

Jamaican

This lively bar-restaurant features the Jamaican-inspired dishes of Cecil Palmer, whom you might have met at his Jazz Fest food booth. Fruity island cocktails and weekend reggae bands bring New Orleans just a little closer to the Caribbean.

✉ **606 Frenchmen St**
☎ **944-4744** ⏱ Tues-Fri 11am-3pm, Tues-Thurs 6pm-midnight, Fri-Sat 6pm-late ♿ **V**

Cafe Sbisa (6, G7) $$$
Creole
Century-old Cafe Sbisa has the glamour of a Hollywood grande dame – a little flash and a lot of grace. The outdoor patio overlooks Decatur St, while the indoor dining room has a view of the Art Deco mural over the bar. The Sunday jazz brunch is also a crowd pleaser.
✉ **1011 Decatur St**
☎ **522-5565** ⏱ **Sun-Thurs 5:30-10:30pm, Fri-Sat 5:30-11pm, Sun brunch 10:30am-3pm** V

Central Grocery (6, G7) $
Deli
The muffuletta was born in 1906 at this busy grocery and deli at the hands of Salvatore Lupo, the Sicilian owner; this famous sandwich combines ham, salami, provolone and olive relish between slices of flat, round muffuletta bread, which is similar to focaccia. Sadly, the sandwiches we tried nearly 100 years later were lackluster and not worth the long wait in line.
✉ **923 Decatur St**
☎ **523-1620** ⏱ **Mon-Sat 8am-5:30pm, Sun 9am-5:30pm** ♿

Clover Grill (6, F6) $
Diner
Want a little 'shake' with those fries? Dancing waiters and pulsating techno tracks heat up the late-night scene at Clover Grill, a diner with a dynamite performance.
✉ **900 Bourbon St**
☎ **598-1010** ⏱ **24hrs**

Coop's Place (6, F7) $
New Orleans/Bar
More a bar than a restaurant, Coop's makes one of the best gumbos in the Quarter and is a sure bet for a relaxed, need-to-feed experience.
✉ **1109 Decatur St**
☎ **525-9053**
⏱ **11am-2am**

Country Flame (6, J4) $
Mexican/Spanish/Cuban
This Mexican dive preserves some of the Quarter's famed seediness. Check out the decommissioned trough under the bar – a dead giveaway of a bygone stand-and-swill saloon.
✉ **620 Iberville St**
☎ **522-1138**
⏱ **11am-10pm**

Court of Two Sisters (6, G5) $$$
Creole
If you want all of New Orleans' signature dishes at your command, then come here for the daily jazz brunch. Sample over 80 dishes, from boiled crawfish to shrimp rémoulade, on the pleasant wisteria-shaded patio. The food quality is passable, but at least you won't die wondering.
✉ **613 Royal St**
☎ **522-7261** ⏱ **9am-3pm, 5:30-10pm** ♿

Eggs over easy: Clover Grill

Croissant d'Or Patisserie (6, F7) $
Café/Bakery
Behind the scenes at this beautifully tiled bakery, toqued chefs are hard at work making fresh croissants and French pastries. The coffee is as thick as molasses, and the pastries' sugar spike delightful.
✉ **615-617 Ursulines Ave** ☎ **524-4663**
⏱ **7am-5pm**

Café Du Monde – serving beignets to the masses

Elizabeth's (2, C2) $
New Orleans
Elizabeth's hearty sand-wiches and down-home breakfasts deliver on the rumor that good food lies ahead. The endangered Creole breakfast dish called *calas*, deep-fried rice balls dusted in powdered sugar, can be ordered here.
✉ **601 Gallier St**
☎ **944-9272** 🚖 **cab or drive** ⏲ **Tues-Sat 7am-2:30pm** ⛄

Evelyn's Place (6, J4) $
New Orleans/Deli & Bar
Evelyn's doesn't see much action until late night when the service-industry crowd wanders in. During the day, you've got the place to yourself for a simple meal of red beans and rice, Pabst Blue Ribbon from the tap and a few tall tales from your new old pal, Frank.
✉ **139 Chartres St**
☎ **522-2216** ⏲ **11am-late**

Feelings Cafe (2, C2) $$$
Creole
You may have heard that Feelings is *the* place to go for a romantic dinner. If you're undecided, don't go. If you're already convinced, then go informed. Make reservations for the upstairs balcony, which is the *only* romantic spot. Go hungry and get sauced to disguise that the food is mediocre.
✉ **2600 Charters St**
☎ **945-2222** 🚖 **cab only** ⏲ **Fri-Sat 6-11pm,** Sun-Thurs 6-10pm, lunch/brunch Fri-Sun 11am-2pm

Fiorella's (6, F7) $
New Orleans
Informal Fiorella's is just what a family escaping the Bubba Gump cult is looking for. Done up like a salty fish shack, Fiorella's fries just about anything (chicken, pickles, pies) and has an Italian 'WOP' salad for that pesky vegetarian daughter.
✉ **45 French Market Pl**
☎ **528-9566** ⏲ **Sun-Thurs 7am-midnight, Fri-Sat 7-2am** ⛄ **V**

Flora Cafe (6, E10) $
Café
This neighborhood coffee shop serves as an informal civic center for the Marigny's and Bywater's boho resi-dents. Poetry readings on Monday nights, local art dis-plays and meat-free burritos join the cast of regulars.
✉ **2602 Royal St at Franklin** ☎ **947-8358**
🚖 **5 Marigny/Bywater at Franklin** ⏲ **7am-midnight** ⛄ **V**

Gilberto Gone from Galatoire's
In the spring of 2002, something shocking happened at Galatoire's restaurant: a waiter was fired. Things don't change at Galatoire's, especially not the adored waiters, whose tenure at the restaurant is equal in status (and duration) to a professorship at an Ivy League school. When news of the dismissal filtered through the tight-knit club of regulars, they launched a campaign to reinstate their beloved waiter. In letters and even an unfashionably modern website (**e** www .welovegilberto.com), prominent members of the community detailed grievances against the restaurant as far-reaching as replacing hand-chipped ice with machine-made, relaxing the dress code to attract more tourists and allowing women into the male-dominated waiter culture. A formal boycott of the restaurant has yet to manifest.

Croissant d'Or Patisserie – heaven for pastry lovers

Galatoire's Restaurant (6, H4) $$$
Creole
Of the old-liners, Galatoire's gets the most compliments for its fish and seafood dishes such as shrimp remoulade and trout meuniere amandine. A well-hidden highlight is fried eggplant Galatoire's (dipped in powdered sugar). Reservations required for upstairs; first-come, first-served for downstairs; jackets required.
✉ **209 Bourbon St**
☎ **525-2021** ⏱ **Tues-Sat 11:30am-10pm, Sun noon-10pm**

The Harbor (6, D10) $
Soul
A modest extension of a local bar, The Harbor cooks up soul-food classics, such as fried chicken, turkey wings, and pork chops and gravy. To show you're in the know, order gumbo and potato salad. Don't forget the banana pudding – it's a hot commodity.
✉ **2529 Dauphine St**

Breadwinners
While almost everyone agrees that colonialism was a great tragedy, one must also admit that France introduced the world to a much-needed staple: delicious crusty bread. Louisiana was well trained and today boasts a softer-centered variety than the thin Continental baguette. Oddly, it was late-18th-century German settlers, not French, who cultivated the bread wheat in this area. One survivor, Leidenheimer's Bakery, can be spotted running age-old morning delivery routes throughout the French Quarter.

☎ **947-1819**
🚌 **5 Marigny/Bywater at Franklin**
⏱ **Sat-Thurs 6am-3pm, Fri 6am-5pm** ♿

Irene's Cuisine (6, G7) $$
Italian
The flavors of New Orleans and Sicily are wed amid the romantic environs of this family-owned eatery. House specialties include oysters Irene, duck St Philip and soft-shell crab. Reservations not accepted; no sleeveless shirts for men.
✉ **539 St Philip St**

☎ **529-8811** ⏱ **Sun-Thurs 5:30-10:30pm, Fri-Sat 5:30-11pm**

Johnny's Po-Boys (6, H5) $
New Orleans
Well publicized on a well-worn path, you might dismiss Johnny's as a tourist trap. But its fame only improves the quality. The fried oyster po'boy (lightly breaded in cornmeal) will turn a raw oyster purist into a devotee.
✉ **511 St Louis St**
☎ **524-8129** ⏱ **Mon-Fri 8am-4:30pm, Sat-Sun 9am-4pm** ♿

K-Paul's Louisiana Kitchen (6, H5) $$$
Contemporary Cajun
Wasn't that whole blackened thing just a flash in the pan? Granted, the craze for all things Cajun has cooled, but chef Paul Prudhomme's signature eatery is still a great meal. Longtime favorites include blackened twin beef tenders with debris (gravy) sauce, and turtle soup. Reservations required for upstairs; first-come, first-served for downstairs; business casual.
✉ **416 Chartres St**
☎ **596-2530**
⏱ **Mon-Sat 6-10pm**

Highbrow Cafe Sbisa raises eyebrows

La Peniche (6, D7) $
Breakfast

All sorts of night owls make this Faubourg Marigny breakfast joint a character study in eccentricity. Order waffles with peanut butter, bananas and pecans, with a side of bacon, and you'd have a meal fit for the King (Elvis, that is).

✉ 1940 Dauphine St
☎ 943-1460 🚗 at night cab or drive
🕐 24hrs

Luigi's Fine Foods (6, G7) $
Deli

Just two doors away from Central Grocery, Luigi's has perfected the muffuletta sandwich: the bread is fresher and the olive spread is spicier. Finish with the custardy bread pudding, coated with a tame rum sauce, to cut that post-'muff' breath.

✉ 915 Decatur St
☎ 529-4975
🕐 10am-5pm

Load up your plate at Court of Two Sisters

Lulu's (6, H5) $
Californian

In a city where macaroni and cheese is considered a vegetable, Lulu's largely vegetarian menu seems strangely exotic. Simple and fresh salads, hearty sandwiches and intoxicating desserts head the lunchtime lineup in a space no bigger than a closet and less formal than the corner grocery.

✉ 307 Exchange Alley
☎ 525-2600 🕐 Mon-Sat 10:30am-3:30pm, Fri-Sat 6-9:30pm V

Mona Lisa Restaurant (6, F7) $
Pizzeria

This neighborhood pizza joint offers a safe haven from the crowds and fuss of the Quarter. With knock-off paintings of the famous old broad and soft lighting, Mona Lisa is romantic in that college-first-date way.

✉ 1212 Royal St
☎ 522-6746
🕐 11am-11pm ♿ V

Napoleon House (6, H5) $
New Orleans

In the 1820s, New Orleanians cooked up a plan to liberate Napoleon from exile and transplant him to this house. The story lived longer than the plan, or the emperor for that matter, and adds a dash of fame to a great food bar. The food menu is straightforward New Orleans and can be enjoyed in a candlelit courtyard.

✉ 500 Chartres St
☎ 524-9752 🕐 Mon-Thurs 11am-midnight, Fri-Sat 11am-1am, Sun 11am-7pm ♿

Old Dog New Trick Café (6, E8) $
Vegetarian

Surrounded by lemon yellow retro decor, Old Dog barks at city-savvy vegetarians far removed from the crusty

Expand your empire (or at least your belly) at Napoleon House

hippies of yore. Gourmet salads, sandwiches and Asian-inspired dishes deliver flavor without animal involvement.

✉ 517 Frenchmen St
☎ 943-6368
🕐 11am-10pm ⚱ **V**

Olivier's (6, J5) $$
Creole
Without all the decorum of the old-line restaurants, Olivier's stays true to the Creole commandments while satisfying modern palates. Inheriting recipes from five generations, this family-owned restaurant cultivates a real culinary appreciation with such honestly priced dishes as eggplant Olivier and gumbo sampler.

✉ 240 Decatur St
☎ 525-7734 🕐 11am-3pm, 5-10pm **V**

Peristyle (6, F5) $$$
Louisiana Contemporary
A newcomer to the culinary scene, Anne Kearney produces updated French fare in a clean and romantic space teetering on the edge of the Quarter. Louisiana squab, veal loin with artichokes, and caramelized onion tart are just some of the seasonal offerings; reservations required.

✉ 1041 Dumaine St
☎ 593-9535
🕐 Tues-Thurs 6-9pm, Fri-Sat 6-10pm

Port of Call (6, E6) $
Bar & Grill
The dark Polynesian-themed restaurant consistently receives accolades for its mammoth burgers chaperoned by a baked potato. After a meal here, you'll never be hungry again.

✉ 838 Esplanade Ave
☎ 523-0120
🕐 11am-late ⚱

Enter Emeril's for excellent eating

Quarter Scene Restaurant (6, F5) $$
New Orleans
Tennessee Williams used to frequent this neighborhood restaurant, which does everything from breakfast to New Orleans standards; the jambalaya is a wash, but the pecan catfish keeps promiscuous foodies loyal.

✉ 900 Dumaine St
☎ 522-6533 🕐 Mon-Fri 8am-2pm, 5:30-10pm, Sat-Sun 8am-10pm ⚱ **V**

Tujague's (6, G6) $$
Creole
Crisp white tablecloths, a checkered-tiled floor and a commanding cypress bar create an alluring old-world

ambience. Tujague's (pronounced two-jacks) offers a five-course set menu, including a beef brisket that locals salivate over; reservations recommended.

✉ 823 Decatur St
☎ 525-8676
🕐 11am-3pm, 5-11pm

Verti Marte (6, F7) $
Deli
Take a sharp left after the potato-chip aisle to reach the take-away deli counter. Spicy jambalaya, breakfast and lunch sandwiches and daily chef specials feed those in a hurry.

✉ 1201 Royal St
☎ 525-4767
🕐 24hrs **V**

Dining Solo

The city's incomparable communal spirit will make dining alone less lonely. **Emeril's Restaurant** (p. 78) has a chef's table where solo diners can view the unsung heroes behind the Emeril machine. **Herbsaint** (p. 78) has a small common bar and a wine-tasting menu to loosen a shy diner. The bar seats at **K-Paul's** (p. 75) receive the attention of the friendly bartender, who will navigate newbies through the menu and the wine list. The oyster bar at **Acme** (p. 71) is always a blast.

CBD & WAREHOUSE DISTRICT

Deanie's (5, J8) **$**
New Orleans
Feeling a little peckish after the D-Day Museum? Grab a bite with locals at this no-frills lunch counter, where plate lunches and po'boys won't sink your wallet.
✉ 1016 Annunciation St ☎ 250-4460

🚌 10 Tchoupitoulas at Poeyfarre ⊙ Mon-Fri 7am-3pm ♿

Emeril's Restaurant (5, G8) **$$$**
Louisiana Contemporary
Of Emeril's three restaurants, his namesake flagship is the surest guarantee of a memorable meal. An eclectic menu jumps from Creole sauces to Italian raviolis to straight-shooting Americana. The chef isn't around these days, but his smiling mug can be found on the bathroom tiles. Reservations required; business casual.
✉ 800 Tchoupitoulas St ☎ 528-9393 🚌 10 Tchoupitoulas at Julia St ⊙ Mon-Fri 11:30am-2pm, Mon-Thurs 6-10pm, Fri-Sat 6-11pm

Herbsaint (5, F6) **$$**
Louisiana Contemporary
Named after the local anise liqueur, Herbsaint offers the ultimate in refreshing mid-day dining. Light 'comfort' dishes, such as the daily pasta or steak tartare with *pommes frits*, satisfy hunger as effortlessly as the restaurant's namesake drink satisfies thirst. Dinner reservations recommended; business casual.
✉ 701 St Charles Ave ☎ 524-4114 🚌 St Charles at Girod St ⊙ Mon-Thurs 11:30am-2pm, 5-10pm, Fri-Sat 5-11pm

Horinoya (5, E5) **$$**
Japanese
Although the competition isn't immense, Horinoya easily nudges the other sushi restaurants out of bounds. For a local twist, try *managatsuo miso yaki*, grilled pompano fish marinated in miso.
✉ 920 Poydras St ☎ 561-8914 🚌 St Charles at Poydras ⊙ Mon-Fri 11:30am-2:30pm, 5-10pm, Sat 5-10:30pm, Sun 5-10pm ♿ **V**

Culinary Luminaries

Paul Prudhomme was just a little (well, big boned) country boy from Opelousas, Louisiana, who managed to put his state's cuisine on the national map in the 1980s. As executive chef at Commander's Palace, he developed the now ubiquitous blackened redfish dish. Striking out on his own to found K-Paul's, he led the revolution against the monopoly of family-owned restaurants, paving the way for other chef-driven satellites.

Susan Spicer brings 'nouvelle' to New Orleans with combinations of Asian, European and Indian concepts. Her surprisingly simple dishes shift culinary power from the classic French sauces to the main ingredients. True to her understated ways, she's yet to mix TV celebrity with her restaurant success, first Bayona in the 1990s and now two additional ventures, Herbsaint and Cobalt.

Kickin' it up a notch, chef **Emeril Lagasse** has achieved so much national attention that some fear 'president' Emeril might be the next stop. His empire includes a Food Channel TV program, a failed sitcom, three New Orleans restaurants (NOLA, Emeril's and Delmonico), plus one in Orlando, Florida, and another in Las Vegas. A native of Fall River, Massachusetts (from a French-Canadian and Portuguese family), he too is a graduate of Commander's executive chef position.

Spicy Susan cooks up a storm

Thomas Downs

Lee Circle Restaurant (5, G6) $$$

Louisiana Contemporary
Decorated in a halfhearted attempt at minimalism, the dining room of Hotel Le Cirque's restaurant is as stylish as sackcloth, but the food can't be as easily dismissed. Creamy mirliton (chayote) bisque with crabmeat, oysters and brie and an entree of Gulf seafood will make you salute the general in the middle of the circle; reservations recommended.
✉ 2 Lee Circle ☎ 962-0915 🚋 St Charles at Lee Circle ⏰ Mon-Fri 11:30am-2:30pm, 5:30-10:30pm; Sat-Sun 5:30-10:30pm

Lemon Grass takes your senses to Saigon

Lemon Grass (5, D7) $$

Vietnamese
Amid the blonde chic decor of the International House Hotel, chef Minh Bui pays tribute to his mother's former café in Saigon with lemongrass chicken, shrimp dumplings and home-made organic tofu; dinner reservations recommended; casual.
✉ 217 Camp St, in International House Hotel ☎ 523-1200
⏰ Mon-Fri 11am-2pm, Sun-Thurs 6-10pm, Fri-Sat 6-11pm V

Liborio Cuban Restaurant (5, E8) $$

Cuban
Named after a Cuban version of Davy Crockett, this family-owned restaurant is a popular lunch retreat for young CBD capitalists. *Ropa vieja* (shredded beef with sweet plantains), roast pork and paella are a liberation from the Creole dictatorship; reservations recommended.
✉ 321 Magazine St ☎ 581-9680 🚌 10 Tchoupitoulas at Gravier ⏰ Mon-Sat 11am-3pm, Tues-Sat 6-9pm V

Mother's Restaurant (5, E8) $

New Orleans
Locals gripe that Mother's is an overpriced tourist trap; they're partly right, but it is still fun. Mother's is central and action packed, with a long line, a chaotic ordering system and heart-attack specialties such as the Ferdi po'boy (ham, roast beef, debris and gravy) – yummy.
✉ 401 Poydras St ☎ 523-9655 🚌 10 Tchoupitoulas at Poydras ⏰ Mon-Fri 6:30am-10pm, Sun 7am-10pm ♿

Sno balls

Finely shaved ice with gobs of sickeningly sweet syrup poured over the top make the beginnings of New Orleans' favorite nonalcoholic treat: the sno ball. What distinguishes the sno ball from the nationally recognized snow cone is the spirit of experimentation. Rarely is a sno ball just one flavor; combos run from complementary (lemon and lime) to confrontational (root beer and lemonade). The addition of ice cream or cream flavors turns flavored ice into flavor bombs. Start a career of sno-ball exploration at SnoWizard Sno-ball Stand (4001 Magazine St; 3, H10), Hansen's Sno-Blitz (4801 Tchoupitoulas St; 3, J8; ☎ 891-9788), or Royal St Sno-balls (cnr of Royal & St Ann Sts; 6, G6).

Praline Connection
(5, H8) $$
Soul
Two blocks from the convention center, Praline Connection stirs the soul with barbecued ribs, fried chicken and a Sunday gospel brunch. A praline candy shop and second location on Frenchmen St testify to the restaurant's success.
✉ 907 S Peters St
☎ 523-3973 🚌 10
Tchoupitoulas at St Joseph St ⏰ Mon-Fri 11am-3pm, Sun 11am-1pm & 2-4pm ♿

Restaurant August
(5, E8) $$$
Louisiana Contemporary
Creole cuisine gets a German interpretation from native son John Besh, at this converted tobacco warehouse. Baked oysters coated in horseradish and soft brioche crumbs, and herb-rubbed duck transport the spoils of the hunt to the modern table.
✉ 301 Tchoupitoulas St ☎ 299-9777
⏰ Mon-Fri noon-2pm, Mon-Sat 6-10pm

Restaurant Cuvée
(5, E8) $$$
Louisiana Contemporary
Classy Cuvée's repertoire introduces Creole to other regional and international cuisines. Sugarcane smoked duck breast with seared Hudson Valley foie gras and pear glace could follow a prelude of crispy mirliton and spicy shrimp Napoleon. Reservations recommended; business casual.
✉ 322 Magazine St
☎ 587-9001 🚌 11
Magazine at Gravier St
⏰ Mon-Fri 11:30am-2:30pm, Mon-Thurs 6-10pm, Fri-Sat 6-11pm
Ⓥ

Oyster Cult
Baked, grilled, raw, deep fried, thrown in gumbo, made into soup – New Orleans has found 1001 delicious recipes for these mollusks.

Old-line restaurants always have a house baked-oyster dish. The most nationally recognized is Antoine's oysters Rockefeller; the rich sauce (hence the John D connection) is made of spinach, breadcrumbs, bacon, spices and anise liqueur and spooned over the half-shelled oysters before baking.

Equally addictive are oysters on the half shell. Raw bars in New Orleans are as revered as old-line restaurants, but are a lot more fun. Common wisdom advises that raw oysters only be eaten during months with the letter 'r' – which excludes the summer months. This may have had more to do with lack of proper refrigeration in the hot weather than with seasonal flaws in the oysters. However, the colder months deliver the sweeter oysters.

Riomar (5, G8) $$
Spanish/Mediterranean
Two blocks from the convention center, this seafood restaurant features dishes from the Spanish mainland as well as its former colonies. Riomar's ceviches amaze New Orleanians who don't know that fish aren't born deep fried. Reservations recommended; business casual.
✉ 800 S Peters St
☎ 525-3474
🚊 Riverfront at Julia St ⏰ Mon-Thurs 11:30am-3pm, 6-10pm, Fri 11:30am-3pm, 6-11pm, Sat 6-11pm Ⓥ

Sweet Olive Cafe
(5, F8) $
Café
This simple lunch counter assembles creative sandwiches and salads that fuel the downtown workday crowd.
✉ 610 Tchoupitoulas St ☎ 299-8188 🚌 10
Tchoupitoulas at Lafayette ⏰ Mon-Thurs 9am-3pm, Fri 9am-2pm Ⓥ

Vic's Kangaroo Café
(5, F8) $
Bar & Grill
A walk from the convention center, this Australian-owned outpost does *dinkum Aussie tucker* (real Australian food) as well as familiar New Orleans and pub grub.
✉ 636 Tchoupitoulas
☎ 524-4329 🚌 10
Tchoupitoulas at Girod St ⏰ Mon-Fri 11:30am-3am, Sat-Sun 6pm-3am

Restaurant August

GARDEN DISTRICT, UPTOWN & RIVERBEND

All Natural Foods & Deli (5, H6) $
Vegetarian
At the deli in the back of this upper Magazine St health food store, you can get big fresh salads with the dressing on the side. Vegan sandwiches, steamed greens and smoothies will recalibrate you for another round with New Orleans' rich cuisine.
✉ 5517 Magazine St
☎ 891-2651
🚌 11 Magazine at Napoleon ⏰ Mon-Thurs 10am-7pm, Fri-Sat 10am-6pm, Sun 10am-5pm ♿ **V**

Bluebird Cafe (3, G11) $
Breakfast
Start your morning the way God intended with a heap-

The chef is on top of his game at Brigtsen's

ing helping of short-stack pancakes or Belgian-style waffles in dizzying varieties: traditional, buckwheat, butter pecan, banana, blueberry and silver dollar.
✉ 3625 Prytania St
☎ 895-7166 🚌 St Charles at Amelia St
⏰ Mon-Fri 7am-3pm, Sat-Sun 8am-3pm ♿

Brigtsen's Restaurant (3, B2) $$
Creole
In a romantic little house surrounded by begonias and shady trees, chef Frank Brigtsen can coax a game lover from a cowardly eater. Savor saying his specialty: rabbit tenderloin on a tasso (cured pork or beef) Parmesan grits cake with sauteed spinach and a Creole mustard sauce.
✉ 723 Dante St
☎ 861-7610 🚌 St Charles at Maple
⏰ Tues-Sat 5:30-10pm

Camellia Grill (3, C2) $
Diner
Only in New Orleans would a greasy spoon come packaged in a Greek-revival minimansion. As plain as the pink neon sign, Camellia Grill serves the late-night musicians and early morning sightseers diner favorites, as well as signature milkshakes and decadent chocolate pecan pies; cash and traveler's checks only.
✉ 626 S Carollton Ave
☎ 866-9573 🚌 St Charles at S Carrollton
⏰ Mon-Thurs 9am-1am, Fri 9am-3am, Sat 8am-3am, Sun 8am-1am ♿

Save the Vegetables
Thanks to New Orleans' proximity to bodies of water, vegetarians who eat fish will have an easy culinary trip. For the vegetable-lover or stricter vegetarian, the road will be pretty rocky. New Orleanians consider the only good vegetable to be a fried one. Salads cause even more contempt and come wilted, aging and drowned in dressing.

Unassuming **Lulu's** (p. 76), on Exchange Alley, is a little piece of California's whole-food scene in the French Quarter. A bit further afield, **All Natural Foods & Deli** (p. 81), on upper Magazine St, offers vegan options. Organic and vegetarian grocery items can be collected at **Whole Foods Market** (3135 Esplanade; 4, G4; ☎ 943-1626), in Esplanade Ridge. The store also carries Serious ice cream, a local brand with mouthwatering flavors such as burnt sugar and blackberry.

For locally grown vegies, boiled peanuts and local color, head to the **Crescent City Farmers Market**, which is held at Uptown Square (200 Broadway St; 3, F2) on Tuesday 10am-1pm and in the Warehouse District (700 Magazine St; 5, F7) on Saturday 8am-noon.

Casamento's (3, H9) $
New Orleans
Since 1949 this Uptown institution has figured prominently in many families' dinner routines. In this immaculately clean, gleaming tiled interior, you'll wonder if you've gone to 'raw bar' heaven; checks and cash only.
✉ **4330 Magazine St**
☎ **895-9761** 🚊 **11 Magazine at Napoleon Ave** ⏰ **Tues-Sun 11:30am-1:30pm, 5:30-9pm; closed summer**

Commander's Palace (3, F13) $$$
Creole
Neatly coiffed ladies in their jewel-toned Sunday best file into Commander's, a Garden District old-liner dating from the 1880s. Paul Prodhomme and Emeril Lagasse ran the kitchen before defecting to solo projects. Commander's gets loads of praise, especially for its turtle soup with sherry, bread-pudding souffle, and Sunday brunch. Reservations required; try for the upstairs parlor or Garden Room; jackets required.
✉ **1403 Washington Ave** ☎ **899-8221** 🚊 **St Charles at Washington Ave** ⏰ **11:30am-1:30pm, 6-8:30pm**

Late-Night Eats
Oops! You did it again – it's now 3am and you're hungry (and probably drunk). What's a New Orleans tourist to do? Follow Bourbon St past the strip clubs and bead shops to **Clover Grill** (p. 73), where a diner-sized disco sizzles in the wee hours. **Camellia Grill** (p. 81), in Riverbend, is another hallowed hall of diner insomniacs.

Verti Marte (p. 77), a French Quarter deli, is open 24hrs and will deliver all sorts of salty goodness to your hotel or bar stool.

If late-night doesn't equal greasy burger, **Belle Forché** (p. 72) serves Creole fusion dishes until 2:30am at weekends.

Cooter Brown's Tavern & Oyster Bar (3, C2) $
Bar & Grill
Raw oysters and a four-page beer menu – yee-haw, pah-ner! Better plan on staying awhile if you make the trek to this Riverbend college haunt.
✉ **509 S Carrollton Ave** ☎ **866-9104** 🚊 **St Charles at S Carrollton** ⏰ **Mon-Thurs 11am-3am, Fri 11am-4am, Sun 11am-2am**

Dante's Kitchen (3, B2) $$
Contemporary Louisiana
Steps from the Mississippi in a cozy 1860s cottage, Dante's creates honest food such as grilled shrimp BLT sandwiches for lunch, falafel-crusted fish for dinner, and sweet potato pie for dessert. Catch the streetcar away from the crowds to enjoy a Sunday brunch on the garden patio; dinner reservations required.
✉ **736 Dante St** ☎ **861-3121** 🚊 **St Charles at Maple St** ⏰ **11:30am-2:30pm, 5:30-10pm** **V**

Domilise's Po-Boys (3, J5) $
New Orleans
It's a mouthful, but locals swear by the hot smoked sausage po'boy with chili gravy and Creole mustard. Domilise's is in the riverside section of the Garden District; cash only.
✉ **5240 Annunciation St** ☎ **899-9126** 🚗 **cab or drive** ⏰ **Mon-Sat 11am-7pm** ♿

Dunbar's (3, E7) $
Soul
Why is Dunbar's popular? It's not the neighborhood, which is way Uptown and on the crummy side. Oh that's right, it's the all-you-can-eat red beans and rice and fried-chicken lunch special. See ya there.
✉ **4927 Freret St** ☎ **899-0734** 🚗 **cab or drive** ⏰ **Mon-Sat 7am-9pm**

If you can't stand the heat, try Casamento's raw bar

Franky & Johnny's
(5, J5)   **$**
New Orleans
When it is crawfish season,
go straight to this down-
home joint and get yourself
a platter of the boiled bug-
gers. Any other time of the
year, don't even bother trying to find this place;
everything we tried tasted
strangely like old grease.
✉ **321 Arabella St**
☎ **899-9146**
🚌 **10 Tchoupitoulas
at Arabella**
⏰ **11am-10pm ♿**

Jacques-Imos
(3, A2)   **$$**
Creole/Southern
This casual joint is so
popular with locals that
they'll gladly drink away a
few hours waiting for a
table. Shrimp and alligator
sausage cheesecake, cala-
mari, crawfish etouffee
and fried chicken top the
greatest-hits list. Big
groups turn the place into
a real madhouse and solos
or couples will feel a little
abused; reservations
accepted only for groups
of 5 or more.
✉ **8324 Oak St**
☎ **861-0886** 🚌 **St
Charles at Oak** ⏰ **5:30-
10pm; closed Aug**

Juan's Flying Burrito
(3, F15)   **$**
Mexican
Lower Garden District hip-
sters sustain their lean
artistic look at this cheap-
eats joint. Buoy that old-
fogey feeling by ordering a
gutter punk burrito – yeah,
you used to be a rocker.
✉ **2018 Magazine St**
☎ **569-0000** 🚌 **11
Magazine at Sophie
Wright Place** ⏰ **Mon-
Sat 11am-11pm, Sun
noon-10pm ♿ V**

Lilette (3, H11)   **$$$**
French
High hopes are pinned on
former Bayona chef John
Harris's ability to keep the
nouvelle New Orleans
cuisine-scape interesting.
Crispy duck confit and
sweet-corn broth with avo-
cado and crabmeat do the
trick nicely. This neighborhood bistro is better
explored as a lunchtime
break from shopping on
Magazine St than a dinner
excursion.
✉ **3637 Magazine St**
☎ **895-1636** 🚌 **11
Magazine at Antoinine**
⏰ **Tues-Thurs 11:30am-
2pm, 6-10pm, Fri-Sat
11:30am-2pm, 6-11pm**

Mat & Naddie's
(3, A2)   **$$**
Louisiana Contemporary
This funky word-of-mouth
place, where Freret St
meets the river, is like step-
ping into a good friend's
home, with family photos
and college-era decor-
ations. At weekends, they
grill oysters right on site.
During the week, they
cook up wacky combos
such as oysters Rockefeller
pizza and black-bean bar-
becue shrimp; dinner reser-
vations recommended.
✉ **937 Leonidas St**
☎ **861-9600** 🚌 **cab
or drive** ⏰ **Tues-Fri
11am-2pm, Tues-Sat
5:30-9:30pm V**

Seasoned locals know it's worth the wait at Jacques-Imos

Parasol's Restaurant & Bar (3, G13) $

New Orleans/Bar
Many missing husbands can be found clustered around the bar at this Irish Channel favorite, a block off Magazine St. The loyal following boasts that the roast-beef po'boy beats any other in town.
✉ 2533 Constance St
☎ 899-2054 🚋 St Charles at Third St
🕐 11am-10pm

Tee-Eva's Creole Soul Food (3, H9) $

Creole/Soul
This squat yellow building with cartoonlike happy faces painted on it makes you smile even before you order an individual sweet potato pie or praline from the take-away window. The woman behind the name used to sing backup for the late Ernie K-Doe, a New Orleans celebrity.
✉ 4430 Magazine St
☎ 899-8350
🚋 11 Magazine St at Napoleon
🕐 11am-7pm ♿

Upperline Restaurant (3, G8) $$$

Louisiana Contemporary
Pungent smells of rosemary and lantana greet you at this quirky Uptown restaurant. The three-course sampler menu includes, among other dishes, delectable Louisiana oyster stew with Pernod, and duck with ginger-peach sauce. Save room for some delicious key lime pie for dessert. Reservations required; business casual.
✉ 1413 Upperline St
☎ 891-9822 🚋 St Charles at Upperline St
🕐 Wed-Sun 5:30-9:30pm

Worth a Trip

Just getting out of the French Quarter might be a real chore for most short-term visitors. If it is only for one meal, take a cab or drive to one of these beloved institutions *outside* the Quarter. For oysters and seafood, **Casamento's** (p. 82) and **Uglesich's** (p. 84) deliver both with a side of local charm. **Domilise's** (p. 82) famous po'boys have gained almost mythical status. **Commander's Palace** (p. 82), in the Garden District, has fine dining, pedigree and turtle soup to its credit. Jazz fans will want to pay a visit to **Dooky Chase Restaurant** (p. 86), which served all the visiting African-American musicians during segregation; Dooky's is across from a beleaguered stretch of housing projects, so use inner-city common sense. **Liuzza's by the Track** (p. 86) is just good, beer-soaked fun.

Uglesich's (3, C14) $

Seafood
In an abandoned neighborhood, crammed into a little shack, this is the lunch joint you've heard about. Renowned for fried-seafood po'boys, Uglesich's flexes its muscles in the fresh-catch department; ask at the counter for recommendations. The early bird gets a table, or at least a wait by the 'raw bar' (where you can order oysters on the half shell). Cash only; reservations not accepted.
✉ 1238 Baronne St
☎ 523-8571 🚗 cab or drive only 🕐 Mon-Fri 11am-2pm

Winnie's Artsy Cafe, USA (3, H11) $

Eclectic
Wondering if New Orleanians eat gumbo every day? Some undercover work in this café on Magazine St revealed that locals are just as slaphappy about foreign cuisine as the rest of the country. Italian, Asian and Greek flavors have been imported into these health-conscious grilled sandwiches and wraps.
✉ 3454 Magazine St
☎ 899-3374 🚋 11 Magazine at Louisiana Ave 🕐 Wed-Fri 8:30am-3pm, Sat 8:30am-5pm, Sun 8:30am-4pm ♿ V

Wake up and smell the flowers at Upperline Restaurant

MID-CITY, FAIR GROUNDS & CITY PARK

Angelo Brocato's
(4, H2) $
Ice Cream
For a hot climate, New Orleans has a surprising deficit of native ice-cream shops. Filling the void in the Sicilian tradition is this Mid-City sweet stop, next door to Café Indo. Home-made ice cream comes in such flavors as cantaloupe, ginger ale and lemonade.
✉ 214 N Carrollton Ave ☎ 486-0078
🚌 40, 44 at N Carrollton; at night cab or drive ⏰ 9.30am-10pm daily ♿

Cafe Degas (4, G4) $$
French
This charming outdoor café serves basic Parisian-style fare such as terrines, quiches and salad Nicoise. This is a very cosmopolitan finish to a day at nearby New Orleans Museum of Art.
✉ 3127 Esplanade Ave
☎ 945-5635 🚌 48 Esplanade at Ponce de Leon St ⏰ Tues-Fri 11:30am-2:30pm, Sat 11:30am-3pm, Sun 10:30am-3pm, Tues-Sun 6-10pm ♿

Pretend you're in Paris at Cafe Degas

Café Indo (4, H2) $$$
French-Asian
In a charmless storefront, Café Indo will surprise you with nutty spring rolls, fresh bouillabaisse and spicy curries. The rose-petal ice cream will impart a sublime glimpse into the aromatic life of a honey bee. Reservations recommended; casual.
✉ 216 N Carrollton St
☎ 488-0444 🚌 40, 44 at N Carrollton; cab at night ⏰ Tues-Fri 11:30am-2pm, Tues-Sun 6-9:30pm

Dooky Chase Restaurant: there's a whole lotta love in Leah Chase's soul food

That gourmet feelin' goes stealin' down to your shoes at Restaurant Indigo

Dooky Chase Restaurant (4, J5) $$
Soul/Creole

Ray Charles sang about it; Sarah Vaughan liked the soft-shell crab; Lena Horne preferred the fried chicken. A lot of famous African Americans have come through that door, especially when segregation barred them elsewhere. Even today, they're still coming because kind-hearted Leah Chase puts a lot of love into her Southern and Creole dishes – you can taste it too.

✉ 2301 Orleans Ave
☎ 821-0600 🚗 cab or drive only ⏰ Sun-Thurs 11:30am-10pm, Fri-Sat 11.30am-midnight

Gabrielle (4, G4) $$$
Louisiana Contemporary

A husband-and-wife team runs this small operation, credited as being the anchor for the recently christened 'Gourmet Gully' neighborhood. Oysters Gabi (with artichokes, pancetta, spices and Parmesan) and crawfish enchilada are indeed exciting twists. Don't overlook the dessert menu.

✉ 3201 Esplanade Ave
☎ 948-6233 🚌 48
Esplanade at Ponce de Leon St ⏰ Tues-Sat 5:30-10pm, Fri 11:30am-2pm

Liuzza's by the Track (4, G4) $
New Orleans

Does anyone in this town have a job? Not by the looks of the Liuzza's crew, drinking beer out of chilled goblets and tearing into bowls of seafood gumbo and barbequed shrimp po'boys. In the New Orleans lexicon, barbequed shrimp isn't barbecued but sauteed in butter and garlic (don't tell them that the rest of the world has another meaning).

✉ 1518 N Lopez
☎ 943-8667 🚌 48
Esplanade at Ponce de Leon St ⏰ Mon-Fri 11am-8:30pm, Sat 11am-4:30pm

Restaurant Indigo (4, H5) $$$
Creole

A stunning plantation-style dining room accented with garden-motif brass work breathes new life into a restaurant culture too dependent on the shabby chic look. Dishes contain ingredients assembled from near and far for a luxurious (if a tad *über*-gourmet) experience. Reservations recommended; business casual.

✉ 2285 Bayou Rd
☎ 947-0123 🚌 48
Esplanade at Ponce de Leon St ⏰ Fri 11:30am-2pm, Sun 11am-2pm, nightly 6-10pm

Southern Lobster

You've seen his likeness on magnets and aprons, and if your visit is timed just right you can get chummy with Louisiana's unofficial mascot – no, not Emeril – the crawfish. A native swamp dweller, the crawfish is about three inches long and was credited with founding the universe, according to Native American mythology. Since then its accomplishments have been quite small: the crawfish industry generates about $125 million annually and employs roughly 7000 people in the state. Frozen tail meat is available year-round and is typically used in etouffee, gumbo and the like. But mid-February to June is crawfish season, and the little guys get thrown whole into a pot of boiling water, seasoned with cayenne pepper and other spices until bright red, and then served to a smiling public. Virgins will need a demo on getting at the sweet tail meat, and most servers are happy to oblige. Just remember a simple mantra: pinch da tail, suck da head. Easy, huh?

entertainment

From monthlong citywide parties to 24hr bars, New Orleans loves a good time. It's given birth to a million cocktails, as classy as the Sazerac and as campy as the kamikaze. Alcohol is such a fundamental part of the culture that it is perfectly legal to escort a plastic 'go cup' of booze to your next destination.

Visitors stumble most easily into the year-round Mardi Gras on Bourbon St, loaded with daiquiri stands, cover-band dance clubs and strip joints. The jam-packed party is a great one-night stand, but slinking back for a second night will leave you with a tinge of postcoupling blues.

Thankfully, the Crescent City has cradled a modern generation of musicians bottle-fed on jazz and R&B. Old-fashioned instruments like the trumpet and tuba aren't just relegated to high-school marching bands or stuffy concert halls as in other US cities. Brass instruments are adored, having never been deposed by rock's electric guitar. And in the simple music clubs, five-piece bands cram onto little stages, with the audience only a trombone's slide away. The closeness creates an instant community demonstrating New Orleans' strongest talent – making people feel at ease.

For listings of upcoming shows, refer to the free monthly guides *Offbeat* and *Best of New Orleans* or the weekly *Gambit*. The *Times-Picayune's* Friday entertainment section is called 'Lagniappe.'

Since there isn't a city-enforced closing time, bars stay open as long as there are customers; some never close their doors. In New Orleans your nights could easily blur into your days.

The Jimmy Thibodeaux Band cranks it up on Bourbon St

SPECIAL EVENTS

January

Sugar Bowl – Jan 1; two of the nation's top-ranked college football teams spar in the Superdome

Twelfth Night – Jan 6; the Carnival season kicks off with costume parties and parades

February

Mardi Gras Day – Feb or early March; Fat Tuesday marks the finale of the Carnival season

March

Black Heritage Festival – second weekend; African-American contributions to food, music and the arts are recognized (☎ 827-0112)

St Patrick's Day – March 17; the Lenten penitence is broken with a day of revelry

Tennessee Williams Literary Festival – end of March; five days of literary events celebrate the work of this Southern playwright (☎ 581-1144)

April/May

French Quarter Festival – second weekend of April; twelve stages throughout the French Quarter showcase New Orleans music

Jazz Fest – late April or early May; music, food, crafts and fun occupy the city's social calendar for 10 days

Spring Fiesta – five days in April or May; private historic homes are opened to the public (☎ 581-1367)

July

Essence Music Festival – Independence Day weekend; *Essence Magazine* sponsors star-studded performances at the Superdome

August

Satchmo Fest – Aug 2-4; music and lectures honor the birthday of New Orleans' favorite son Louis Armstrong (☎ 522-5370)

September

Southern Decadence – Labor Day weekend; a gay, lesbian and transgender festival, including a leather block party (☎ 522-8049)

October

Halloween – Oct 31; a giant costume party, Anne Rice Vampire Lestat Extravaganza and monster bash – it's party time again

November

All Saints Day – Nov 1; many residents honor their deceased family members by sprucing up local cemeteries; visitors are welcome

December

Christmas New Orleans Style – monthlong; lights and decorations adorn St Charles Ave, City Park and the lobby of the Fairmont Hotel; many restaurants offer *réveillon* dinners (traditional Creole Christmas Eve dinners) on Christmas Eve (☎ 522-5730)

Feux de Joie – Dec 24; 'fires of joy' light the way along the Mississippi River levees

New Year's Eve – Dec 31; Baby New Year is dropped from the roof of Jackson Brewery at midnight

BARS & DANCE CLUBS

Cafe Brasil (6, E8)
Music and conversation spill out on to the street at this Frenchmen St club. With a bright breezy attitude, Cafe Brasil peddles itself as a 'global human music box' featuring Latin, jazz, reggae and acoustic bands.
✉ **2100 Chartres St**
☎ **949-0851** ⏲ **Sun-Thurs 6pm-2am, Fri-Sat 6pm-4am** 💲 **$5**

Carousel Bar (6, J4)
Another in the revolving bar genre, the Carousel Bar, on the 1st floor of the Hotel Monteleone, makes a complete revolution in about 15mins. The center bar is canopied by the top hat of the 1904 world's fair carousel complete with running lights, hand-painted figures and gilded mirrors. The amber-colored Vieux Carré, a distant cousin of the Manhattan, is its house cocktail, although some bartenders grumble that nobody really likes it.
✉ **214 Royal St**
☎ **523-3341** ⏲ **11am-late** 💲 **no cover**

Circle Bar (5, H6)
Smack-dab on Lee Circle, this cozy bar shelters a cast of regulars. An eclectic mix of bands play weeknights and weekends.
✉ **1032 St Charles Ave**
☎ **588-2616** 🚃 **St Charles at Lee Circle** ⏲ **4pm-4am** 💲 **weekend cover $5**

The Columns Hotel
(3, F10) The closely trimmed lawn and buxom veranda of this civilized watering hole evoke visions of white-suited colonels

sweating alongside their highball glasses of rye whiskey. In real life the outdoor tables are a grand place to toast *laissez-faire* New Orleans. As a sidenote, the Columns hosted the filming of Louis Malle's *Pretty Baby* movie.
✉ **3811 St Charles Ave**
☎ **899-9308** 🚃 **St Charles at General Taylor St** ⏲ **3pm-late** 💲 **no cover** ♿

Coop's (6, F7)
This no-frills, beer-swilling joint has a late-night kitchen and a decent selection of local beer (try Abita's Purple Haze). Bits of deep-fried alligator meat dipped, at your discretion, in spicy Creole mustard make the perfect swamp-inspired munchie food.
✉ **1109 Decatur St**
☎ **525-9053** ⏲ **10am-late** 💲 **no cover** ♿

Cooter Brown's Tavern & Oyster Bar
(3, C2) This college-crowd hangout serves over 400 different beers, many of which are imports. Check

out the 'Beersoleum & Hall of Foam,' a gallery of plastered busts of famous celebrities matched thematically with beers. Peter Sellers nurses a French Fischer LaBelle and Jimmy Cagney guzzles a Harp, but I'll have what Einstein's having.
✉ **509 S Carrollton Ave** ☎ **866-9104**
🌐 **www.cooter browns.com** 🚃 **St Charles at S Carrollton Ave** ⏲ **11am-late** 💲 **no cover**

Cosimo's (6, E6)
For wine lovers with too many beer buddies, Cosimo's is a nice compromise. Cooled by lazy ceiling fans, this elegant neighborhood pub has a generous wooden bar, a fine wine selection and Sunday drink specials. French Quarter locals stop in to wet their whistles after a romp with their pooches in the nearby park.
✉ **1201 Burgundy St**
☎ **522-9715** ⏲ **4pm-late** 💲 **no cover**

Bourbon St – a great place for crowd surfing

The Dungeon (6, H5)
Descend the stone stairs into this gothic lair for midnight dancing or ghoulish cocktails. Three bars, live DJs and lots of Anne Rice mysticism keep the night dwellers properly fed.
✉ **738 Toulouse St**
☎ **523-5530** e www .originaldungeon.com
◷ **midnight-late**
⑤ **$5**

Ernst Cafe (5, F8)
Near the convention center, Ernst relies heavily on the happy-hour office crew and conventioneers but delivers a lot of French Quarter charm with its outdoor tables beside a cobblestone street.
✉ **600 S Peters**
☎ **525-8544**
e www.ernstcafe.net
🚕 **cab or drive** ◷
Mon-Sat 11am-late, Sun 3pm-late ⑤ **no cover**

Fiorella's (6, F7)
This salty fried-food shack might single-handedly revolutionize the game of bingo. In the dingy backroom, both a band named Bingo, composed of a violin and an organ, and the game of bingo, replete with prizes, meet for some friendly crossfire.
✉ **1136 Decatur St**

☎ **528-9566** ◷ **7am-midnight or 2am**
⑤ **cover for bingo night $3-5** ♿

Fritzel's (6, G5)
When Bourbon St is really cranked up, somehow Fritzel's remains an oasis of calm. A wide selection of German beers and liqueurs and a steady stream of real live European tourists might be the French Quarter's closest connection to the Continent. The German owner claims, without remorse, to have first introduced Jaegermeister to the USA. Jazz bands play weekend nights.
✉ **733 Bourbon St**
☎ **561-0432** ◷ **1pm-late** ⑤ **no cover**

Hi-Ho Lounge (6, C9)
Peek into the off-kilter lives of Marigny bohemians at this ratty neighborhood bar. Nearly nightly shows feature alternative punk bands, performance art, folk music or bluegrass acts. The exhibitionist band Morning Federation 40 learned to play their instruments here.
✉ **2339 St Claude Ave**
☎ **947-9344** e www .hiholounge.com 🚕 **cab or drive** ◷ **8pm-late**
⑤ **under $5**

Lafitte's Blacksmith Shop

Lafitte's Blacksmith Shop (6, F6)
Without a lick of paint, this historic bar tilts ever so slightly to one side. When the weather cooperates, the shuttered windows are thrown open to allow tropical breezes to penetrate the cool dark space. Local lore claims that the pirate Jean Lafitte laundered his profits from illegal slave trading through a blacksmithing business on this site.
✉ **941 Bourbon St**
☎ **523-0066** ◷ **noon-late** ⑤ **no cover**

Le Chat Noir (5, F6)
Slick Le Chat Noir celebrates cocktails and theatrics in its CBD digs. In the front piano bar, wide-mouthed martinis are sipped and swilled by happy-hour wage slaves and Edith Piaf sympathizers. The adjoining theater hosts cabaret musicals, political satire and off-color monologues.
✉ **715 St Charles Ave**
☎ **581-5812** e www .lechatnoir.citysearch .com 🚋 **St Charles at Julia St** ◷ **Tues-Sat 6pm-late; show times vary** ⑤ **tickets for shows $16-20; no cover for bar**

Playing Solo
You won't be alone for long if you wander into a bar by yourself in New Orleans. The city's natural friendliness is unleashed like a hurricane after a few drinks and will range from polite curiosity to unwanted flirtation to outright annoyance. Solo women might experience more attention than desired and making friends with the bartender is a good psychological shield. At most music clubs, socializing ends once the band starts, so to avoid drunken Romeos plan to arrive about an hour after the published start time to accommodate for New Orleans 'time.'

Loa (5, D7)

The hotel bar of fashionable International House Hotel, Loa is a great place to grab a daytime drink. The huge picture windows overlook the CBD's streetscape of dedicated worker bees not fortunate enough to be on holiday. At night a strangely Gap-ad crew assembles in the too-khaki interior.

✉ **221 Camp St**
☎ 553-9550 e www
.ihhotel.com ⏰ 5pm-late ⑤ no cover

Lucy's Retired Surfer's Bar & Restaurant (5, F8)

A popular after-work playground, Lucy's brings a little bit of Baja to New Orleans. Pink pussycats (Stoli, Chambord and a surfer secret), 32oz margaritas and Mexican food keep things hangin' loose.

✉ **701 Tchoupitoulas St** ☎ 523-8995
e www.lucysretired
surfers.com 🚕 cab or drive ⏰ 11am-late ⑤ no cover

Molly's at the Market (6, F7)

This epicenter of the Irish expat community sponsors a raucous St Patrick's Day bash. Any other time of the year, share a pint with the resident stiffs: former owner Jim Monaghan and 'Irving' reside in their respective urns behind the bar. Irving just appeared one day on the bar's doorstep sometime around 1980 and, try as you might to make him, he doesn't open up about his past. On Thursdays, local journalists and politicians warm the bar stools.

✉ **1107 Decatur St**
☎ 525-5169 ⏰ 10am-6am ⑤ no cover

Toast of the Town

New Orleans is not only famous for inventing a variety of cocktails, it supposedly invented *the* very first cocktail. In an apothecary on Royal St, the distinguished AA Peychaud mixed his patented bitters with cognac brandy in egg cups, called *coquetiers* in French or 'jiggers' in English. Eventually slurred to 'cocktail,' a new American pastime was born. In this creative spirit, the city went on to concoct or perfect other alcoholic recipes, including the following classics.

Pimm's cup (Pimm's, lemonade, 7-Up and a cucumber slice) – Napoleon House (p. 91)

Mint julep (ice, mint, bourbon) – The Columns Hotel (p. 89)

Hurricane (fruit punch mix, rum) – Pat O'Brien's (p. 92)

Sazerac (whiskey, syrup, Herbsaint, Peychaud's bitters) – Sazerac Bar (p. 92)

Ramos gin fizz (gin, sour mix, half-and-half, orange blossom water) – Sazerac Bar (p. 92)

Vieux Carré (rye whiskey, cognac, sweet vermouth, Benedictine and bitters) – Carousel Bar (p. 89)

Napoleon House (6, H5)

Napoleon really missed out on a good time. Unbeknownst to the exiled emperor, some scheming New Orleanians, including the mayor, wanted to rescue him from St Helena and set him up in this handsome French Quarter building. He died before the plot ever set sail. Bow-tied waiters, martial classical music and dramatic pictures of the emperor arouse uncontrollable urges to have another drink. Try the refreshing Pimm's cup, an English favorite typically found wherever lawn sports are played.

✉ **500 Chartres St**
☎ 524-9752 e www
.napoleonhouse.com
⏰ Mon 11am-5pm, **Tues-Thurs 11am-midnight, Fri-Sat 11am-1am, Sun 11am-7pm** ⑤ **no cover**

Green with Absinthe

A 19th-century urban legend tells the story of a Northerner visiting New Orleans who stops into one of the city's many Sazerac bars. After his first drink, he announces that Sazerac is a drink with integrity. His second helps him realize that the South is incredibly misunderstood. After the third he is a converted rebel and begs the bartender for change in Confederate money.

Perhaps it was this story that cinched the prohibitionists' derogatory opinion of absinthe. A strong herbal liqueur, absinthe gained a grand following in France and New Orleans and was traditionally served with diluted sugar or in cocktails like the Sazerac. The herbal ingredient of wormwood, not absinthe's high alcohol content, was witch-hunted for causing madness (as demonstrated by the ghastly behavior of the Southern sympathizer), and all wormwood products were outlawed in the USA in 1912.

The Sazerac cocktail, however, still survives today. Like an aging rock band, Sazerac just replaced washed-up ingredients with younger faces: brandy was traded for whiskey, and absinthe for Herbsaint, a locally produced anisette. Peychaud's bitters is the one surviving member.

Old Absinthe House

(6, H4) In the 1870s this sweaty Bourbon St fixture was one of the city's many bars serving absinthe, a greenish herbal liqueur now outlawed in the US. Legal stand-ins, such as Pernod or Herbsaint, still make an appearance in the absinthe frappe and other cocktails of the era. But for $7 a cocktail, one would hope for swankier surroundings or at least a Steve Miller–free zone.
✉ **240 Bourbon St**
☎ **523-3181** e **www .oldabsinthehouse.com**
◷ 11am-late ⑤ no cover

Parasol's (3, G13)

This neighborhood sports bar is packed day and night with athletics fiends – even the golf crowd is welcomed. Strangely, though, the TVs are not much to cheer about, further proof that this crew is escaping the old lady and household chores.
✉ **2533 Constance St**
☎ **897-5413** 🚕 cab or drive ◷ 11am-10pm
⑤ no cover

Pat O'Brien's (6, G5)

Home of the hurricane, a dastardly strong rum punch, Pat O'Brien's has more tourist appeal than the city's art museum. And for good reason: these hurricanes are yummy and real ass-kickers. Before you know it, you'll have consumed enough confidence juice to commandeer the piano from the professional. If settling in for the night, do the circuit from the sing-along piano bar to the outdoor courtyard.
✉ **718 St Peter St**
☎ **525-4823** e **www .patobriens.com**
◷ 10am-4am ⑤ no cover

Port of Call (6, E6)

Polynesian-style cocktails named after natural disasters wash down Port of Call's beloved burgers. A seasoned crowd of drinkers usually get 'one for the road' before cocktail hour's quitting time.
✉ **838 Esplanade Ave**
☎ **523-0120** e **www .portofcallneworleans .com** ◷ 11am-late
⑤ no cover ♿

RC Bridge Lounge

(3, D15) This lower Magazine St bar has cast off its motorcycle gang affiliations and emerged as a cool, pet-friendly space that makes a mean mojito. The crowd doesn't filter in until late night.
✉ **1201 Magazine St**
☎ **299-1888** 🚕 cab or drive ◷ 4pm-late
⑤ no cover

St Joe's Bar (3, H6)

Of all the houses of worship to St Alcohol, this Uptown spot is the only one to offer heavenly style with down-to-earth attitude. The dark front room broods with carved wooden crosses and salvaged church pews, while the back patio meditates on a more Asian-inspired sanctuary.
✉ **5535 Magazine St**
☎ **899-3749** 🚕 cab or drive ◷ 5pm-late
⑤ no cover

Sazerac Bar (5, C6)

Legend has it that the bullet-sized dent in the wall was a failed attempt

on Huey Long's life. No doubt he was drinking a highball of Sazerac or perhaps the bar's other signature drink, the Ramos gin fizz; business casual.
✉ **Fairmont Hotel, 123 Baronne St** ☎ 529-7111 e www.fairmont neworleans.com ⏰ Mon 11am-5pm, Tues-Thurs 11am-midnight, Fri-Sat 11am-1am, Sun 11am-7pm ⑤ no cover

Shim Sham Club
(6, H5) You know a locals' scene by the number of bicycles parked out front. Sure enough, Shim Sham is a favorite with the Betty Paige haircuts and rockabilly boys. An eclectic jukebox of bygone hits, glittery Naugahyde booths and an old cigarette machine give the illusion of stylish days of yore. Drag queens and glam rockers come out for cheap Pabst Blue Ribbon on '80s Saturday nights; don't miss the Sunday night cabaret show.
✉ **615 Toulouse St** ☎ 299-0666 e shimshamclub.com ⏰ 2pm-6am ⑤ $5-15

Spotted Cat **(6, E8)**
You could start a night of music- and club-hopping at laid-back Spotted Cat. Early shows of jazz and blues mix perfectly with predinner cocktails. The Cat has created a suitably feminine version of the martini: chocolate- and fruit-infused. (Nick Charles would roll over in his grave.)
✉ **623 Frenchmen St** ☎ 943-3887 e www. thespottedcat.com ⏰ 2pm-late; shows start at 6:30pm ⑤ no cover

360 Bar **(5, E9)**
The ear-popping elevator ride up the spine of the World Trade Center will deliver you to a George Jetson–style revolving bar with panoramic city views. The view of the stunning crescent bend of the Mississippi is well worth the price of a cocktail or two. If the humidity is low, Lake Pontchartrain will eventual come into sight too. On weekend nights, the bar transforms into an upscale dance club with house, techno and hip-hop DJs.
✉ **2 Canal St** ☎ 595-8900 ⏰ Mon-Wed 11am-2am, Thurs-Sat 11am-4am ⑤ DJ nights $10

TwiRoPa **(2, E8)**
Deep in the heart of an abandoned warehouse district, there's a spray-painted sign hung from a broken-down truck pointing to a wretched-looking old rope factory. This is the hottest late-night dance club in town. Tall thin beauties, contortionists, mime artists and heavy star power orbit through 100,000 sq feet of dance space.
✉ **1544 Tchoupitoulas St** ☎ 587-3777 e www.twiropa.com 🚕 cab or drive ⏰ 11pm-late ⑤ $15-20

Vic's Kangaroo Café
(5, F8) A mostly 30s crowd imbibes at this Australian-themed neighborhood bar in the Warehouse District.
✉ **636 Tchoupitoulas St** ☎ 524-4329 e www .satchmo.com/vics 🚕 cab or drive ⏰ Mon-Fri 11:30am-3am, Sat-Sun 6pm-3am; shows at 10pm ⑤ no cover

Whiskey Blue **(5, E8)**
The W Hotel's lobby bar tries so hard to be New York City but it only reaches Newark. It does a few things right: the cobalt-blue back-lit bar, common standing tables and secret-sharing settees set a hip mood. Then the premillennium dance tracks and the flimsy martini glasses smack of discount chic. Young singles searching for someone don't seem to mind a bit.
✉ **333 Poydras St** ☎ 207-5016 ⏰ 11am-late ⑤ no cover

Glam it up at Shim Sham Club's '80s night

MUSIC CLUBS

Donna's Bar & Grill

(6, F5) Across the street from Armstrong Park, Donna's is a true neutral ground between the white French Quarter and the black Tremé. Amid the decor of a worn lunch counter, the brotherhood of music and neighborhood invites a diverse audience to temporarily join their family. As the night wears on, other musicians returning home from sets drop by for impromptu jam sessions. On Monday nights, free red beans and rice and barbecued chicken feed folks between sets.

✉ 800 N Rampart St
☎ 596-6914 e www
.donnasbarandgrill.com
🕐 shows at 11pm
💲 $10

Dos Jefes Uptown Cigar Bar

(3, J5) Take all the trappings of an upscale bar – imported cigars, fine wine and single malt Scotch – and combine it with the ambience of your childhood rec room. Now you've got unpretentious Dos Jefes. Not convinced yet? How about free jazz nightly, killer happy-

hour specials and above average bar food?

✉ 5535 Tchoupitoulas St ☎ 891-8500 🚖 cab or drive 🕐 4pm-late
💲 no cover

El Matador

(6, F8) So hip it hurts, El Matador embodies the post-punk spirit of lower Decatur St. The stage hosts nightly need-to-be-disbanded bands ranging from whiner rock to cacophonous brass. Locals maintain that the flamenco dance show is fun.

✉ 504 Esplanade Ave
☎ 569-8361 🕐 Tues-Wed 9pm-late, Thurs-Mon 5pm-late 💲 $5

Daytime Music

When it comes to catching great live music, the early bird is out of luck. Most bands don't get started until 11pm or later and really start to cook as the next day rolls in. For the daytime dwellers, the buskers on Jackson Square and at the cafés near the French Market are talented musicians, who also perform in many of the clubs at night. In fact, local celebrity Kermit Ruffins got his start playing the streets of the French Quarter with his high-school buddies. Daytime or evening shows can be seen at **Jimmy Buffett's Margaritaville Cafe** (p. 95), the **Spotted Cat** (p. 93), the **Palm Court Jazz Cafe** (p. 96) and the venerable **Preservation Hall** (p. 96).

Funky Butt on Congo Square

(6, F4) The Butt is more sexy than funky, with mobster mood colors and intimate tables arranged adoringly around the musicians. Named after a Buddy Bolden tune, Funky Butt attracts a more modern edge of the jazz crowd, but straight-up swingers are still a fixture.

✉ 714 N Rampart St
☎ 558-0872 e www
.funkybutt.com 🕐 7pm-late 💲cover $5-15

House of Blues

(6, J5) Oddly, it was this national chain that halted the decline of French Quarter live music into crack renditions of 'Play that Funky Music White Boy.' National legends like Dolly Parton and Etta James have played the same stage as local blues and rock talent. An annex club, The Parish, hosts smaller local acts. Happy hours, DJ nights and Sunday gospel brunch widen HOB's appeal.

✉ 255 Decatur St
☎ 529-2583 e www
.hob.com 🕐 8pm-2am,

Donna's Bar & Grill – where chicken and brass unite

Sun gospel brunch
9:30am-4pm ⑤ $8-50 ⚐

Howlin' Wolf (5, H9)
This Warehouse District
music club started out
promoting local pro-
gressive rock bands,
expanded to attract national groups and diversified to
include jazz and blues.
Local funk bassist George
Porter Jr, Frank Black (former lead singer of the
Pixies) and Monday night
amateurs make this one of
the city's best mid-sized
venues.
✉ 828 S Peter St
☎ 522-9653 e www
.howlin-wolf.com
🚗 cab or drive
🕐 show times vary
⑤ $5-15

**Jimmy Buffett's
Margaritaville Cafe
(6, F7)** Margaritaville is a
long way from the Big
Easy, isn't it? Turns out the
New Orleans branch of the
parrot-head cult isn't pure-
ly rampant commercialism.
Jimmy Buffet came here as
a kid to meet up with his
grandfather, a steamship
captain, and later started
his music career here.
Daytime bands, usually
R&B and blues, are an
excellent way for early-to-
bedders to catch live
music.
✉ 1104 Decatur St
☎ 592-2565 e www
.margaritavillecafe.com
🕐 11am-midnight;
shows at 3pm
⑤ no cover ⚐

*Grab the bull by the horns
at El Matador*

Music Week

New Orleans has so much live music that making a choice can be debilitating.
Don't fret, there is a well-traveled music circuit that first-time visitors should hop
on for an introduction. Before long you'll know all the jazz musicians and will be
able to plot your own course.

- Monday – Donna's Bar & Grill (p. 94) for Bob French & Friends (brass)
- Tuesday – Maple Leaf Bar (p. 96) for Rebirth Brass Band (brass)
- Thursday – Vaughan's (p. 97) for Kermit Ruffins & Barbecue Swingers (trad
  jazz/swing), or Mid-City Rock 'n' Bowl (p. 96) for Rosie Ledet (zydeco)
- Friday – Le Bon Temps Roulé (p. 96) for Henry Butler (jazz & R&B piano), or
  Snug Harbor (p. 97) for Ellis Marsalis (jazz piano)

Schedules change and musicians go on tour, so check the monthly entertainment
guide *Offbeat* to confirm suggested shows. On Wednesday, Saturday and Sunday,
there is a grab bag of options; scan the listings for the names mentioned above
or these powerhouses:

- Jason Marsalis (jazz drums)
- Snooks Eaglin (R&B guitar)
- Don Vappe (trad jazz)
- Wild Magnolias (Mardi Gras Indians/funk)
- Los Hombres Calientes (Latin jazz)
- Marva Wright (R&B vocals)
- Treme Brass Band (trad second-line brass)
- Joe Krown (organ jazz)
- Davell Crawford (R&B piano)
- John Boutte (R&B vocals)

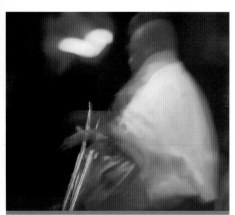

Preservation Hall – the New Orleans jazz institution

Le Bon Temps Roulé

(3, H8) In any other city, this college favorite would host crappy Dave Matthews cover bands. But this is New Orleans and even frat boys adore the power of brass. Pool tables, six nights of music and free Friday night oysters – not a bad college recruitment tool.

✉ 4801 Magazine St
☎ 895-8117
ℯ www.lebontemps
roule.com 🚗 cab or drive ⏱ 4pm-late
⑤ no cover

Lion's Den

(4, J3) New Orleans' very own queen of soul, Irma Thomas, performs at this club when she's in town (which isn't terribly often). With a little advance preparation, you're sure to catch one of her shows here during Jazz Fest. At other times of the year it's a low-key bar.

✉ 544 S Broad Ave
☎ 821-3745 🚗 cab or drive ⏱ 4pm-late ⑤ no cover; ticket prices vary during Jazz Fest

Maple Leaf Bar (3, A2)

An incredible ensemble of local musicians rescues this Uptown bar from college-dive mediocrity. Nightly shows of New Orleans brass, funk, ragtime and R&B with a shot of Georgia corn whiskey go down smooth and easy.

✉ 8316 Oak St
☎ 866-5323 music line, 866-9359 bar
🚗 cab or drive
⏱ 3pm-late ⑤ $8

Mid-City Rock 'n' Bowl (4, J1)

A music show at a bowling alley might sound closer to the skids than a lounge act at an airport hotel. But Rock 'n' Bowl really does rock, and it really is a bowling alley. The blues, zydeco and R&B acts are top of their game, and at their feet there's plenty of elbow room for mere mortals. The weekly zydeco shows have become a steady diet for two-steppin' fanatics.

✉ 4133 S Carrollton Ave ☎ 482-3133
ℯ www.rocknbowl.com
🚗 cab or drive ⏱ daily shows at 10pm ⑤ $8-10

Palm Court Jazz Cafe

(6, F7) Traditional and Dixieland jazz bands play this elegant supper club near the French Market. You can also catch some tunes from the bar area.

✉ 1204 Decatur St
☎ 525-0200
ℯ www.palmcourt
cafe.com ⏱ Wed-Sun restaurant 7-11pm, music 8-11pm ⑤ $5 ♿

Preservation Hall

(6, G5) A veritable museum of traditional and Dixieland jazz, Preservation Hall is an obligation, but it's not guaranteed fun. Crammed into a simple room with limited bench seating, no air-conditioning and no refreshments, serious jazz-heads as well as music morons gather to listen to gray-haired musicians politely sail their instruments. Get in line early to get a seat.

✉ 726 St Peter St
☎ 522-2841
ℯ www.preservation
hall.com ⏱ shows at 8:30pm & 9:30pm
⑤ $5 ♿

Go wild at Lion's Den

Snug Harbor (6, E8)
The traditional-style stage at this Frenchmen St jazz club hosts such luminaries as Ellis Marsalis playing with his son and drummer Jason Marsalis, R&B vocalist Charmaine Neville, and the modern jazz quartet Astral Project; reserve tickets in advance, business casual. The adjoining bar and bistro draws an older crowd than other clubs on the strip.
✉ 626 Frenchmen St
☎ 949-0696 e www
.snugjazz.com ⏲ shows at 9pm & 11pm
⑤ $12-20

Tipitina's (3, J9)
Founded in honor of New Orleans celebrity Professor Longhair (and named after his 1953 hit), Tipitina's was *the* home of 1970s R&B, with regular performances by the Neville Brothers and the Meters. Having lost a little of its edge to savvier competitors, Tipitina's still draws a funky mix of local and national talent, such as Bruce Daigrepont and Sonic Youth, respectively.
✉ 501 Napoleon Ave
☎ 895-8477 box office, 897-3943 concert line e www.tipitinas.com 🚗 cab or drive ⏲ Mon-Fri 11am-6pm ⑤ $8-20

Vaughan's (2, C9)
This quiet little Bywater bar reaches boiling point on Thursday nights, pushing Friday mornings, when trumpet player Kermit Ruffins and his Barbecue Swingers get to work. In between sets, Kermit graciously dishes out barbecued chicken to the crowd. Come for a late, late night since Bywater time is a few hours behind New Orleans time.
✉ 800 Lesseps St
☎ 947-5562 🚗 cab or drive ⏲ open 11am-3am; shows at 11pm Thurs ⑤ $7-10

Innovations in wallpaper at Tipitina's

PERFORMING ARTS

Le Petit Théâtre du Vieux Carré (6, H6)
One of the oldest theater troupes in the country, Le Petit performs a variety of Southern-flavored plays. The long-running *Late Night Catechism* features a cast of nuns cracking Catholic jokes. Stage-adapted fairy tales and standard musicals also fill the schedule.
✉ 616 St Peter St
☎ 522-2081 e www
.lepetittheatre.com
⏲ afternoon and evening shows ⑤ $21-26/8 ⚹

Louisiana Philharmonic Orchestra (5, D6)
Led by music director Klauspeter Seibel, the orchestra is one of only two musician-owned symphonies in the world. An instrument 'petting zoo' precedes special family programs. The symphony performs at the downtown *Orpheum Theater* (129 University Place; 5, C6), and the annual season runs from September through May.
✉ 305 Baronne St
☎ 523-6530 e www

.lpomusic.com
⑤ tickets $11-36, reduced tickets for family events ⚹

Southern Repertory Theatre (6, K5)
The moody, and sometimes disturbing, stories of famous Southern playwrights, such as Tennessee Williams and Carson McCullers, practically fall into your lap at this intimate theater of only 150 seats.
✉ 3rd fl, 333 Canal Pl
☎ 522-6545
e www.southernrep.com ⑤ $20/15 ⚹

CINEMAS

Canal Place Cinemas
(6, K5) Part of the Landmark Theaters chain, this multiplex fills a cinema void with a super-convenient location. Features include Hollywood darlings along with industry outsider movies.
✉ 3rd fl, 333 Canal Pl
☎ 581-5400 ⑤ $10/5 ☥

Entergy IMAX Theatre
(5, D10) Amazon caves, haunted castles and space exploration get supersized on the 5½-story screen in the surround-sound theater. Part of the Audubon Nature Institute complex, the theater is next to the Aquarium of the Americas, and combination tickets are available.
✉ 1 Canal St ☎ 581-4629 e www.audubon institute.org ⑤ $8/5 ☥

Prytania Theatre
(3, G6) For a city its size, New Orleans doesn't have much of an active art-house scene. Independent and other ugly duckling movies get the royal treatment at this antique moviehouse, which claims to be one of the last remaining single-screen theaters in the state and was built in 1900.
✉ 5339 Prytania St
☎ 891-2787 e www .theprytania.com
🚊 St Charles at Jefferson Ave
⑤ $6.50/4.50 ☥

GAY & LESBIAN NEW ORLEANS

Bourbon Pub and Parade Disco
(6, G5) The party spills out onto the sidewalk at this popular dance and video club. Fans claim the dance floor and light show are better here than across the street at OZ. You can always do comparison shopping.
✉ 801 Bourbon St
☎ 529-2107 ⊙ 24hrs
⑤ cover $5

Good Friends
(6, F5) The crowd of regulars *really* are good friends, partly because the bar stools are so damn comfortable. By far the prettiest bartenders are here making the bar's famous drink, the separator (Kahlua ice cream, milk, brandy and coffee liqueur). The upstairs piano area heats up with show tunes on Sunday nights.
✉ 740 Dauphine St
☎ 566-7191 e www .goodfriendsbar.com
⊙ 24hrs ⑤ no cover

Kim's 940
(6, F8) One of the city's few lesbian bars, Kim's 940 in Faubourg Marigny runs Thursday drink specials, weekend DJs and Proud Marys, a local band. If you get too drunk to drive, stay at Kim's guesthouse.
✉ 940 Elysian Fields Ave ☎ 944-4888
e www.kims940.com
🚕 cab or drive
⊙ 4pm-late ⑤ cover $5-10

OZ
(6, G5) Even Uptown debs have shaken their tail feathers at this mixed dance club. The pump-and-grind area is surrounded by a cast-iron balcony and the bar is manned by buff, shirtless bartenders. Sounds like Thanksgiving at granny's.
✉ 800 Bourbon St
☎ 593-9491 ⊙ 24hrs
⑤ cover $5

Rawhide 2010
(6, F5) Leather in the morning, leather in the evening, leather at suppertime. Behind those dark windows, you'll find well-groomed men wearing leather.
✉ 740 Burgundy St
☎ 525-8106 e www .rawhide2010.com
⊙ 24hrs ⑤ no cover

Where everybody knows your name

THEATERS & LARGE VENUES

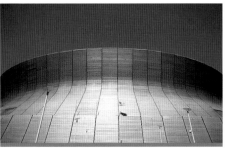

Louisiana Superdome – the world's largest sugar bowl

Contemporary Arts Center (5, G7)

The anchor for the Warehouse District's art community, CAC sponsors modern plays and dance performances. Musical shows have included tributes to Jimi Hendrix and Cuban jazz. The center also hosts the annual New Orleans Film Festival.

✉ **900 Camp St**
☎ **523-1216** ℮ **www .cacno.org** 🚋 **St Charles at Lee Circle**
⑤ **$8-20** ♿

Louisiana Superdome (5, D3)

Resembling a huge exhaust vent, the Louisiana Superdome reaches 27 stories high and encompasses 125 million cubic ft of space. During football season, the New Orleans Saints play their home games in this indoor stadium. Every year the Sugar Bowl college football is held here, and professional league Super Bowls return to the stadium an average of every four years. Big, big, big names, such as the Rolling Stones and the Pope, are able to fill the dome's capacity.

✉ **1500 Sugar Bowl Dr**

☎ **587-3810**
℮ **www.superdome .com** 🚗 **cab or drive**

Mahalia Jackson Theatre of the Performing Arts (6, E4)

Named in honor of the great gospel singer Mahalia Jackson, this theater houses the renowned New Orleans Opera and Ballet Association.

✉ **Armstrong Park**
☎ **565-7470**

New Orleans Arena (5, E3)

The Arena's sugar daddy is the Hornets, a pro basketball team. During the off-season, music groups stop here during big multi-city tours. Highlights have included Cher's aptly named 'Living Proof – the Farewell Tour,' the second of her farewell tours to play the Arena.

✉ **1501 Girod St**
☎ **587-3824 tickets, 846-5959 information**
℮ **www.neworleans arena.com**
🚗 **cab or drive**

Saenger Theatre (6, H3)

Big names such as Jerry Seinfeld and Bill Cosby as well as touring Broadway musicals appear at this grand 1920s theater.

✉ **143 N Rampart St**
☎ **524-2490 box office, 522-5555 tickets** ℮ **www.sae ngertheatre.com**
🚗 **cab or drive**

Saenger Theatre – for a little culture between cocktails

SPECTATOR SPORTS

Football

The National Football League's **New Orleans Saints** play nine home games from August through December at the **Louisiana Superdome** (p. 99). The Saints march in but rarely march out victorious. Many fans attribute this losing streak to the Superdome's misfortunate location over an old cemetery. Several years ago, a well-respected voodoo priestess was brought in to break the curse; the antidote only lasted one game.

The hottest college football ticket is the New Year's **Sugar Bowl**, featuring the Southeastern Conference champions.

Basketball

In 2002 New Orleans wooed the National Basketball League's Hornets team, formerly located in Charlotte, North Carolina. The season runs from October to April.

Baseball

The New Orleans Zephyrs, a minor league baseball team, is affiliated with the Houston Astros. The season runs from April to September.

Horseracing

One of North America's oldest racetracks, the **Fair Grounds Race Track** hosts thoroughbred racing from Thanksgiving through March. In the spring, Jazz Fest turns the fair grounds into a marathon of music and merriment.

Louisiana Superdome

Offices & Venues

Tickets for most professional sports events are handled by Ticketmaster (☎ 800-877-0898; **e** ticketmaster.com).

New Orleans Saints (1500 Sugar Bowl Dr; 5, D2; ☎ 731-1700; **e** www.new orleanssaints.com; tickets $35-80)

Sugar Bowl (1500 Sugar Bowl Dr; 5, D2; ☎ 525-8573; **e** www.nokiasugar bowl.com; tickets $60-100)

New Orleans Hornets (5, D2; ☎ 525-4667; **e** www.nba.com/hornets; tickets $20-80)

New Orleans Zephyrs (6000 Airline Dr, Metairie; ☎ 734-5155; **e** www.zephyrs baseball.com; tickets $5-9)

Fair Grounds Race Track (1751 Gentilly Blvd; 4, G4; ☎ 944-5515; **e** www .fgno.com; tickets $1-4)

places to stay

Greater New Orleans has over 32,000 hotel rooms; most visitors stay in the French Quarter, right on Bourbon St, although the drawback is seeing the aftermath of the previous night's party. The Quarter's outer fringe is the best compromise: it's close, but not too close, to the action.

An equally charming option is the tree-lined Esplanade between the river and N Rampart St – it's walking distance to the Quarter and to the hip clubs on Frenchmen St. Crossing N Rampart, lakeside Esplanade has many affordable historic B&Bs, ideal for Jazz Fest but not as convenient to the Quarter.

In the CBD, high-rise hotels – from boutique to classic corporate

Room Rates

The categories indicate the cost per night of a standard double room in high season.

Deluxe	$300 and up
Top End	$200-299
Mid-Range	$100-199
Budget under	$99

– accommodate business travelers and conventioneers. Farther upriver, the Garden District is a good base for Mardi Gras – many parades travel down St Charles Ave, where there's large hotels catering to groups and families and offering shuttle service to the Quarter and the convention center. Friendly B&Bs in galleried homes are ideal for romancing couples or business travelers escaping sterile chain hotels. Otherwise, the neighborhood, however beautiful, is a little too residential for most visitors.

The high demand for rooms in the Quarter ensures you won't get what you pay for: mid-range rooms are really budget quality, with well-worn furnishings and musty air-conditioning. Things improve as you move up the price scale and out of the Quarter; most hotels have interior courtyards or exterior balconies and some semblance of Old World charm. Off-street parking typically costs $16 a day at the smaller hotels and $25 and up at the larger hotels.

The city's high season runs from late winter to late spring; business and rates slack off in the morbidly hot summer. All hell breaks loose during special events such as Mardi Gras and Jazz Fest, when rates triple and vacancies shrink to 5%.

No sign of Napoleon at Josephine's eponymous guesthouse (p. 105)

DELUXE

Melrose Mansion
(6, D6) The magazine
Architectural Digest
drooled all over this spec-
tacular 1880s Victorian
mansion – for very good
reason. The four-poster rice
beds, floor-to-ceiling windows, expansive ceilings
and clean masculine fur-
nishings are all a little
dizzying. But power players
and celebrities seem quite
at home here.
✉ **937 Esplanade Ave**
☎ **944-2255; fax 945-
1794** e **www.melrose
mansion.com** ✗ **Port of
Call (p. 77)** ⚹

Omni Royal Orleans
(6, H5) An all-white marble lobby and other palatial
accoutrements pay homage
to the former tenant on this
site, the St Louis Hotel, a
fashionable meeting place
for 19th-century sugar
planters. More marble (a
serious sign of luxury)

makes an appearance in
each room's loo, and
there's a rooftop pool.
✉ **621 St Louis St**
☎ **529-5333; fax 529-
7089** e **www.omni
royalorleans.com** ✗
Rib Room ⚹

Soniat House (6, F7)
This restored Creole townhouse is the perfect place
for a bended-knee pro-
posal or a romantic get-
away. From the street the
small inn's splendor is
camouflaged, slowly unfolding as you step through the
front door into a cool stone
carriageway, leading to a
sunny courtyard greened by
lush palms and banana
trees. A curved, hand-hewn
stairway leads to the galleried rooms decorated in
elegant European antiques.
✉ **1133 Chartres St**
☎ **522-0570, 800-544-
8808; fax 522-7208**
e **www.soniathouse
.com** ✗ **Quarter Scene
Restaurant (p. 77)** ⚹

The best of the best: Melrose Mansion

TOP END

Fairmont Hotel (5, C6)
It's power and scandal –
not furniture polish – that
you smell in the lobby of
the Fairmont. This grande
dame, formerly named the
Roosevelt Hotel, hosted
Huey Long's gubernatorial
bid in 1927 and later
served as his refuge from

Baton Rouge. Modern-day
suites retain some old-
school glamour, but doubles
are a disappointment.
✉ **123 Baronne St**
☎ **529-7111, 800-866-
5577; fax 529-4775**
e **www.fairmont.com**
✗ **Sazerac Bar & Grill** ⚹

**Hotel Inter-
Continental New
Orleans (5, E7)**
The lobby of this CBD
mega-high-rise buzzes with
ringing cell phones, business networking and post-
conference unwinding.
Rooms are well sized and
donned in regular hotel
garb. Local artist George
Schmidt's history of jazz
and Mardi Gras pieces line
the hotel bar walls.
✉ **444 St Charles Ave**
☎ **525-5566; fax 523-
7310** e **www.new-or
leans.interconti.com**
🚊 **St Charles at
Poydras St** ✗ **Veranda
Restaurant** ⚹

I love the smell of upmarket in the morning: the Fairmont

Hotel Monteleone

(6, J4) The oldest and largest hotel in the French Quarter is just as handsome as the day it opened in 1886. The rooms are a little small, but the central location and the spiffy 'I'm-somebody-important' lobby keeps people happy. A young Liberace once played (the piano) on the roof.

✉ **214 Royal St**
☎ 523- 3341, 800-535-9595; fax 528-1019
e www.hotelmonte leone.com ✗ Hunt Room Grill ♿

House on Bayou Road

(4, H5)
This grand Creole cottage sits on a former indigo plantation in the Esplanade Ridge neighborhood. With its extensive gardens, common parlor and Saturday cooking classes, you might find you spend most of your New Orleans visit on the grounds; there are worse places to be. Free parking.

✉ **2275 Bayou Rd**
☎ 945-0992, 800-882-2968; fax 945-0993
e www.houseonbay ouaroad.com 🚌 48 Esplanade at Bayou Rd ✗ Restaurant Indigo (p. 86) ♿

Chains at the Airport

Best Western
☎ 800-528-1234
Doubletree
☎ 800-222-8733
Hilton
☎ 800-872-5914
Radisson Inn
☎ 800-333-3333
Sheraton
☎ 504-885-5700

Hotel Standouts

Boutique bonus – Hotel Monaco (CBD) (p. 105)
Budget beauty – Gentry House B&B (French Quarter) (p. 108)
Creole luxury – Soniat House (French Quarter) (p. 102)
Homey inn – Maison Perrier (Garden District) (p. 106)
Jazz Fest find – House on Bayou Road (Esplanade Ridge) (p. 103)
Mardi Gras guesthouse – Josephine Guesthouse (Lower Garden District) (p. 105)
Mid-range stalwart – Lamothe House Hotel (Faubourg Marigny) (p. 108)
Swank digs – Melrose Mansion (Faubourg Marigny) (p. 102)

Lafayette Hotel

(5, F6) Adjacent to Lafayette Square in the CBD, this small hotel provides a welcome alternative to corporate institutions. Since the hotel has only 44 rooms, the front desk clerk will know your name and you won't have to stand in a line to check in.

✉ **600 St Charles Ave**
☎ 524-4441, 800-525-4800; fax 523-7327
e www.lafayettehotel .com 🚃 St Charles at Lafayette Sq ✗ Herbsaint (p. 78) ♿

W Hotel New Orleans

(5, E8)
Everybody loves the W and its IKEA-like minimalism. Techno music pulsates through the lobby (or 'living room' in W speak); standard-sized rooms sport the trademarked W bed and DSL access. But for all its modern chic, the rooms have an unfashionably musty smell. There is also a French Quarter branch (6, J5).

✉ **330 Poydras St**
☎ 525-9444, 877-946-8357; fax 523-2910
e www.whotels.com
✗ **Zoë Bistrot** ♿

Windsor Court (5, E8)

Queen of the classic corporate hotels, Windsor is crowded with winged chairs, paintings of hunting scenes and perfectly behaved plants. Deluxe rooms are sunny and large with a vanity area, and suites have kitchenettes.

✉ **300 Gravier St**
☎ 523-6000; fax 596-4513 **e** www.windsor courthotel.com
✗ **Mother's Restaurant** (p. 79) ♿

House on Bayou Road

MID-RANGE

Andrew Jackson Hotel (6, F6)

This 22-room guesthouse is a repeat favorite, mainly for its central location and friendly staff. The quality of the rooms can be inconsistent; the ones off the lobby are noisy. Its sister property Hotel St Pierre (6, D5) is even more of a mixed bag. Limited parking.

✉ **919 Royal St**
☎ **561-5881, 800-654-0224; fax 596-6769**
e **www.historicinns neworleans.com**
✕ **Verti Marte (p. 77)** ♿

Avenue Plaza Hotel & Spa (3, E13)

This bustling high-riser is worth investigating for families and large groups, especially during Mardi Gras. All rooms have kitchenettes and can be reconfigured to add space. Free shuttle.

✉ **2111 St Charles Ave**
☎ **566-0198, 800-535-9575; fax 679-7627**
e **www.avenueplaza hotel.com** 🚋 **St Charles at Josephine St**
✕ **Mr John's Steak & Seafood** ♿

Bourbon Orleans (6, G5)

In all honesty, you've got to *really* love Bourbon St and endless repeats of 'Mustang Sally' to want to stay at this nexus of mayhem. This large, modern hotel claims to occupy the site of the famous Quadroon Balls, an antebellum tradition in which well-educated quadroon beauties were introduced to white Creole aristocrats as potential mistresses.

✉ **717 Orleans St**
☎ **523-2222; fax 571-4666** **e** **www.wynd ham.com** ✕ **Café Lafayette** ♿

Chateau Hotel (6, F6)

It is a Herculean task to find a decent mid-range hotel in the French Quarter, but this might be it. Although it seems a cliche, rooms really are clean and well appointed. Free parking.

✉ **1001 Chartres St**
☎ **524-9636; fax 525-2989** **e** **www.chateau hotel.com** ✕ **Clover Grill (p. 73)**

The Columns Hotel (3, F10)

New Orleans' version of a country club, the Columns is a majestic Greek revival building separated from the street by a manicured lawn. Although the exterior screams elitism, the hotel rooms are quite down to earth. The downstairs bar affords a front-row view of Uptown District aristocracy chasing away the daily shakes with a drink.

✉ **3811 St Charles Ave**
☎ **899-9308**
e **www.thecolumns .com** 🚋 **St Charles at General Taylor St**
✕ **Albertine's Tea Room** ♿

Degas House (4, H5)

Edgar Degas stayed in this restored B&B when it belonged to his Creole cousins, the Mousson family; the bottom floor is a museum documenting the painter's visit to New Orleans. Rooms are well sized, with the added bonus of being able to brag that 'Degas slept here.'

✉ **2306 Esplanade Ave**
☎ **821-5009, 755-6730; fax 821-0870** **e** **www .degashouse.com** 🚋 **48 Esplanade at Tonti St**
✕ **Restaurant Indigo (p. 86)** ♿

Hotel de la Monnaie (6, F8)

Across from the Old US Mint, this condo-style timeshare has suites that can sleep four to six people. The building isn't particularly charming, but the rooms afford a lot of elbow room between traveling companions. Limited free parking.

✉ **405 Esplanade Ave**
☎ **947-0009; fax 945-6841** ✕ **Old Dog New Trick Café (p. 76)** ♿

Chains on Canal St

Along busy Canal St, super-sized chain motels have filled the void left by long extinct department stores; the accommodations are reliable and the location is convenient, with the added bonus of anonymity. They include:

Clarion (1300 Canal; 6, H2; ☎ 800-252-7466)
Crown Plaza (739 Canal; 6, J4; ☎ 962-0500)
Doubletree (300 Canal St; 6, K5;.☎ 888-874-9074)
Le Meridien (614 Canal St; 6, J4; ☎ 527-6715)
Marriott (555 Canal St; 6, J4; ☎ 581-5100)
Ritz-Carlton (921 Canal St; 6, H3; ☎ 524-1331)
Sheraton (500 Canal St; 6, J4; ☎ 888-396-6364)
Wyndham (100 Iberville St at Canal Place; 6, K5; ☎ 566-7006)

Mingle with the Uptown elite at The Columns Hotel

Hotel le Cirque
(5, G6) Another in the hip boutique line, this recent newcomer is attired in citrus-colored '60s decor – without the attitude. Rooms are sizable and some overlook Lee Circle: close the blinds to deter that peeping general.
✉ 2 Lee Circle
☎ 962-0900, 888-487-8782; fax 962-0901
e www.hotel lecirque.com
🚋 St Charles at Lee Circle ✕ Lee Circle Restaurant (p. 79) ♿

Hotel Monaco (5, D7)
How refreshing to find a corporate hotel with style: evocative of pre-WWII North Africa, the vaulted tiled entryway leads to a lobby where ceiling fans cut staccato shadows across the marble floors. The well-sized rooms come with fun accessories, including faux-mink throws, a complimentary goldfish and other toys for regressing grown-ups.
✉ 333 St Charles Ave
☎ 561-0010; fax 561-0036 e www.mon aco-neworleans.com
🚋 St Charles at Poydras St ✕ Cobalt ♿

Hotel Provincial (6, F7)
This mid-sized property in a quiet part of the Quarter has period-decorated rooms and European elegance. On the 5th floor you'll get a hearty view of the Mississippi.
✉ 1024 Chartres St
☎ 581-4995, 800-535-7922; fax 581-1018
e www.hotelprovin-cial.com ✕ Croissant d'Or Patisserie (p. 73) ♿

Hotel Storyville
(6, D5) While it lacks the antique charm of some of its neighbors, Hotel Storyville's ordinary furnishings are a relief for the clumsy among us. Suites with kitchens and dining areas sleep two to six people, and there's free parking.
✉ 1261 Esplanade Ave

☎ 948-4800, 866-786-7984; fax 945-7456
e www.hotelstory ville.com 🚋 48 Esplanade at Tremé St ✕ Port of Call (p. 77) ♿

Hotel Villa Convento
(6, F7) This family-owned and -operated hotel has bright, cheery rooms and was once a boarding house to none other than a young Jimmy Buffet.
✉ 616 Ursulines Ave
☎ 522-1793; fax 524-1902 e www.villa convento.com
✕ Croissant d'Or Patisserie (p. 73) ♿

Josephine Guesthouse (3, E14)
You might wrap up a stint at the Josephine feeling as if you had stayed with old friends. The owners (who are fluent in French) have exquisite art collections, ranging from Haitian folk paintings to a Hapsburg ivory-inlaid bed (you're not going to find that at the Ramada). Free parking.
✉ 1450 Josephine St
☎ 524-6361, 800-779-6361; fax 523-6484
e http://www.bbon line.com/la/josephine/index.html 🚋 St Charles at Josephine St ✕ Juan's Flying Burrito (p. 83) ♿

Long-Termers
Vacation Rentals On-Line (e www.vacationrentals online.com) has a database of New Orleans rentals, ranging from condos to houses large enough for seven people. From the company's homepage, choose 'Property Search' to navigate to its New Orleans listings. Oakwood Corporate Housing (☎ 800-259-6914) manages furnished apartments in the CBD and Warehouse District. Corporate apartments are also offered by **Maison Perrier** (p. 106) and **Prytania Park Hotel** (p. 108), both in the Garden District.

Children in Tow

Most places offer flexible room arrangements, from suites that can sleep up to six people to cots or fold-out beds. In New Orleans' hot climate, you and the kids will be thankful for a swimming pool; all but the smallest places in the Quarter and the private homes in other neighborhoods typically have pools and decent-sized courtyards. Other bonuses to consider are balconies and elevators – ask when you make arrangements.

Lafitte Guest House

(6, F6) Decorated with aristocratic furnishings, this French manor house has all the Old World trappings with New World friendliness. The standout rooms include No 5, with a steep spiral staircase to the loft bedroom, and No 40 occupying the entire top floor (with city views).

✉ 1003 Bourbon St
☎ 581-2678, 800-331-7971 e www.lafitte guesthouse.com
✕ Clover Grill (p. 73) ♿

Le Richelieu (6, F7)

A loyal following sings the praises of this mid-sized hotel on the outer edge of the Quarter. While the rooms are a bit tired and lack that New Orleans joie de vivre, the rates are surprisingly reasonable. Free parking.

✉ 1234 Chartres St
☎ 529-2492, 800-535-9653; fax 524-8179
e www.lerichelieu hotel.com ✕ Terrace Café ♿

Maison Perrier (3, G9)

A bit of a trek into the Garden District, this family-owned guesthouse is sociable and relaxed, with Abita beer on tap, afternoon cookies and games for big and little kids. The decor is comfortable, like an average suburban home, and corporate apartments are also available.

✉ 4117 Perrier St
☎ 897-1807, 888-610-1807; fax 897-1399
e www.maisonperrier .com 🚋 St Charles at Marengo St
✕ Casamento's (p. 82) ♿

Maison St Charles Hotel & Suites (3, C14)

On a busy strip of St Charles Ave, this quasi-historic motel/hotel is a great place for families. Large swimming pools and courtyards give the kids lots of space to stretch their legs and lungs. A free shuttle runs to the CBD and French Quarter.

✉ 1319 St Charles Ave
☎ 522-0187, 800-831-1783; fax 529-4379
e www.maisonst charles.com 🚋 St Charles at Thalia St
✕ La Madeleine ♿

Olde Victorian Inn

(6, F5) Once upon a time a Midwestern couple came to New Orleans for their honeymoon and vowed to make the city their home. Voila: an inn is born! Proprietors Keith and André know the pain of being dumb tourists and will steer first-timers to the best of the Big Easy. The inn's six bedrooms are decorated in quasi-Victorian style.

✉ 914 N Rampart St
☎ 522-2446, 800-725-2446 e www.oldevic torianinn.com
✕ Peristyle (p. 77) ♿

Olivier House Hotel

(6, G5) Just around the corner from the Bourbon boogie, this family-owned hotel is a rambling old place with comfortable, versatile rooms that can sleep a duo or a big band. The mattresses are a tad soggy, but the lush courtyards and friendly staff make it a good alternative to the big chains. Free parking.

✉ 828 Toulouse St
☎ 525-8456; fax 529-2006 e www.olivier house.com ✕ Court of Two Sisters (p. 73) ♿

Place d'Armes (6, G6)

Next to Jackson Square, Place d'Armes has a lot going for it with its convenient location and romantic setting. But the windowless rooms and small bathrooms drive visitors to drink too many frozen daiquiris.

✉ 625 St Ann ☎ 800-366-2743; fax 581-3802
e www.placedarmes .com ✕ Cafe du Monde (p. 72) ♿

Hotel Provincial

B&B Brokers

Looking for a more intimate glimpse into New Orleans' grand homes? Try the following B&B brokers who can custom-match you with the right place: **Bed & Breakfast, Inc** (☎ 488-4640, 800-729-4640; **e** www.historiclodging.com), **Bed and Breakfast & Beyond** (☎ 896-9977, 800-886-3709; **e** www.nolabandb.com) and **Louisiana B&B Association** (☎ 225-346-1857, 800-395-4970; **e** www.louisiana bandb.com).

When you book with a B&B, be sure to inquire about bathrooms. Some of the older houses don't always have in-room toilets.

Pontchartrain Hotel

(3, E14) This 75-year-old classic enjoys a sterling reputation based on its name and longevity alone. Rooms, however, are a little musty and the decor is straight out of a hotel manual. Free shuttle, no pool.
⊠ **2031 St Charles Ave** ☎ **524-0581, 800-777-6193; fax 529-1165** **e** **www.pontchartrain hotel.com** 🚊 **St Charles at Josephine St** ✕ **Lafitte's** ♿

A Quarter Esplanade

(6, E7) This pet-friendly hotel has tidy, modern rooms with kitchenettes, and is stumbling distance from the French Quarter and Frenchmen St. Free parking.
⊠ **719 Esplanade Ave** ☎ **948-9328, 800-546-0076; fax 940-6190** **e** **www.quarteresplan ade.com** ✕ **Mona Lisa Restaurant (p. 76)** ♿

Rathbone Mansion Esplanade

(6, D5) A healthy walk from the French Quarter, this informal Greek revival home has hardwood floors, high ceilings and 12 generous-sized rooms, some with balconies. It's pet friendly and there's free parking.
⊠ **1227 Esplanade Ave** ☎ **947-2100, 800-947-2101; fax 947-7454** **e** **www.rathboneinn .com** 🚊 **48 Esplanade at Tremé St** ✕ **Port of Call (p. 77)** ♿

Sun Oak B&B

(6, D8) A real star in the Faubourg Marigny, this two-bedroom B&B gives visitors a rare vista into the modern life of an 1830s Creole cot-tage. With restored architectural details and local artwork, architect Eugene Cizek and artist Lloyd Sensat have captured New Orleans' historic past and its vibrant creative present.
⊠ **2020 Burgundy St** ☎ **945-0322** **e** **www .sunoaknola.com** ✕ **La Peniche (p. 76)** ♿

Terrell House

(3, E15) Do you get lost in those big hotels where everything looks the same? In this lower Garden District home, you'll still be an easy drive from the convention center but surrounded by drop-dead gorgeous antiques and a navigable floor plan. Proprietor Bobby Hogan is a PGA member and can arrange golf packages. Free parking.
⊠ **1441 Magazine St** ☎ **524-9859, 800-878-9859; fax 524-9859** **e** **www.lacajun.com /terrellhouse.html** 🚊 **11 Magazine at Felicity St** ✕ **Juan's Flying Burrito (p. 83)**

What's behind the blue door at Sun Oak B&B?

BUDGET

Avenue Garden Hotel (3, D14)

This newly renovated place is the hotel version of a furniture store: they're slashing their prices to unheard of lows. Seriously though, the rooms are good-looking, and that's not the beer goggles talking.

✉ **1509 St Charles Ave** ☎ **521-8000, 800-379-5322; fax 528-3180** e **www.avenuegarden hotel.com** ⊕ St Charles at MLK Blvd ☆

A Creole House (6, F5)

Got questions about New Orleans and don't want to read this lousy book? Check yourself into this guesthouse near Armstrong Park and bend the ear of Dave, the manager and former tour guide; an annex property was the presumed 19th-century home of voodoo Queen Marie Laveau. Rooms can be inconsistent, so view before accepting.

✉ **1013 St Ann St** ☎ **524-8076, 800-535-7858** e **www .big-easy.org** ✕ Quarter Grocery ☆

Gentry House B&B

(6, F5) Your first apartment might have looked a lot like the rooms at this converted Creole cottage near Armstrong Park; these can morph into a variety of layouts to accommodate large and small groups. Owner Sadie Gentry is a personable host and, true to her English roots, might be found in the garden taking afternoon tea. There's no off-street parking and credit cards are not accepted.

✉ **1031 St Ann St** ☎ **525-4433; fax 525-** 9102 e gentryhse@aol .com ✕ Quarter Scene Restaurant (p. 77) ☆

India House Hostel

(4, J3) Funky India House sports a backpacker attitude rarely found in major US cities. Solo travelers will find a built-in network of friends and revelers hanging out by the pool, dubbed the 'India Ocean', or in the road-weary living room. There's also a laundry on-site for those steamy nights.

✉ **124 S Lopez St** ☎ **821-1904** e **www .indiahousehostel.com** ⊕ 41, 42 or 43 Canal to S Lopez ✕ Liuzza's by the Racetrack (p. 86)

Lamothe House Hotel (6, E7)

Shaded by the live oaks of Esplanade, the Lamothe House wins for shabby gentility. Suites have soaring ceilings and brooding period furnishings, but double rooms are a little cramped. Free parking.

✉ **622 Esplanade Ave** ☎ **944-9700, 800-367-5858; fax 943-6536** e **www.new-orleans .org** ✕ Café Negril (p. 72) ☆

Mazant Guest House

(2, C8) Deep in the Bywater, Mazant is a convivial hostel for solo travelers or those on a small budget. Getting to and from the Quarter might be a drag since the Bywater can be dicey, but urban frontier types will love the neighborhood. Free parking.

✉ **906 Mazant St** ☎ **944-26662** ⊕ 5 Marigny/Bywater ✕ Bywater Bar-B-Que (p. 72) ☆

Prytania Park Hotel

(3, D15) In the lower Garden District, this low-key hotel offers a lot for less. It has warm honey-colored rooms in a restored 1850s guesthouse or more contemporary rooms in an adjacent motel. Corporate apartments are also available.

✉ **1525 Prytania St** ☎ **524-0427, 800-862-1984; fax 522-2977** e **www.prytaniapark hotel.com** ⊕ St Charles at MLK Blvd ☆

Ursuline Guest House (6, F6)

The digs here are pretty straightforward: bed, door, bathroom, lamp. Any questions? Solo travelers rave about the courtyard rooms centered around a hot tub, and the guesthouse welcomes same-sex couples.

✉ **708 Ursulines Ave** ☎ **525-8509, 800-654-2351; fax 525-8408** ✕ Mona Lisa Restuarant (p. 76)

India House Hostel

facts for the visitor

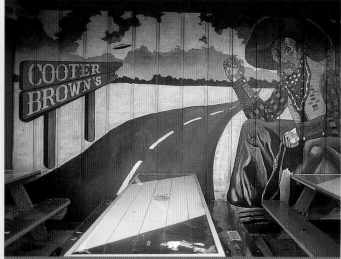

Cooter Browne's Tavern & Oyster Bar – going my way?

ARRIVAL & DEPARTURE

Most visitors arrive by plane at the city's only commercial airport, the Louis Armstrong New Orleans International Airport (MSY). It is mainly a destination airport (not a transfer hub), and flights from Europe will have a stopover in another US city before reaching New Orleans. Flights from Latin America on US-based carriers usually stop in Miami en route to New Orleans; Mexican and South American carriers do offer direct international flights to certain destinations.

Air

Louis Armstrong New Orleans International Airport (2, B2)

The airport is 21 miles west of the city center in the town of Kenner. A single terminal is connected to four concourses. Facilities include a tourist information booth, banks and money exchange, restaurants, bars and telephones.

Left Luggage

There is 24-hour baggage storage available on the lower level of the airport between baggage claims 5 and 6. Contact a baggage coordinator at ☎ 877-847-7172. Lockers are in each concourse.

Information

General Inquiries	☎ 464-0831

Flight Information

Air Canada	☎ 888-247-2262
Aeroméxico	☎ 800-237-6639
American Airlines	☎ 800-433-7300
British Airways	☎ 800-247-9297
Delta domestic	☎ 800-221-1212
Delta international	☎ 800-241-4141
Grupo Taca	☎ 800-535-8780
Jet Blue	☎ 800-538-3583
KLM	☎ 800-374-7747
United domestic	☎ 800-241-6522
United international	☎ 800-538-2929

Car Park Information	☎ 464-0204

Hotel Booking Service
New Orleans Convention & Visitors Bureau ☎ 566-5003, 800-672-6124; e www.neworleanscvb.com

Airport Access

Public ground transportation from the airport isn't convenient. For one person or two people with little time to spare, a taxi is the best bet. If time isn't an issue, opt for a cheaper shuttle bus. For large groups, a taxi becomes an expensive option.

Public Bus The Louisiana Transit Company (☎ 818-1077) runs public buses from the airport to Airline Hwy (US 61) and along Tulane Ave in the lakeside section of town for $1.50. Take the No 39 Tulane bus to get to downtown for $1.25.

Airport Shuttle The Airport Shuttle (☎ 522-3500) will deliver you from the airport to your hotel for $10/20 one-way/round-trip. The only inconvenience is that you won't be the only passenger and will fall into a queue for hotel drop-off.

Taxi A taxi ride from the airport costs a flat rate of $28 for one to two passengers. Each additional passenger costs another $12.

Bus

Greyhound (☎ 800-231-2222) is the only long-distance bus company serving the South. Buses and trains share New Orleans' Union Passenger Terminal (1001 Loyola Ave; 5, F2&3).

Train

Amtrak (☎ 800-872-7245) trains arrive at Union Passenger Terminal (1001 Loyola Ave; 5, F2&3; ☎ 528-1610). Three trains go through New

Orleans: *City of New Orleans* from Memphis, Tennessee to Chicago; *Crescent Route* from New York City, through Washington, DC, and Atlanta; *Sunset Limited* from Miami to Los Angeles.

Car

The major east-west route to New Orleans is I-10. From points north, I-55 and I-59 both feed into I-10. Hwy 90 delivers drivers south of the city into the Cajun bayous and north into the River Road plantations. To get to the North Shore communities, cross Lake Pontchartrain via the 24-mile causeway.

Travel Documents

Passport
With the exception of Canadians, who need only proper proof of Canadian citizenship, all foreign visitors to the USA must have a valid passport. Your passport should be valid for at least six months longer than your intended stay in the US. Documents proving financial stability and/or guarantees from a US resident are sometimes required, particularly for visitors from Third World countries.

Visa
A reciprocal visa-waiver program applies to citizens of certain countries who may enter the USA for stays of 90 days or less without having to obtain a visa. At the time of publication those countries were Andorra, Australia, Austria, Belgium, Brunei, Denmark, Finland, France, Germany, Iceland, Ireland, Italy, Japan, Liechtenstein, Luxembourg, Monaco, the Netherlands, New Zealand, Norway, Portugal, San Marino, Singapore, Slovenia, Spain, Sweden, Switzerland, the UK and Uruguay.

The most common visa is a non-immigrant visitor visa, B1 for business purposes, B2 for tourism or visiting friends and relatives. For more information, visit the website of the Immigration and Naturalization Service (e www.ins.gov).

Return/Onward Ticket
You must have a round-trip ticket from an airline participating in the visa-waiver program; you must have proof of financial solvency and sign a form waiving the right to a hearing of deportation; and you will not be allowed to extend your stay beyond 90 days.

Customs

Non-US citizens are allowed to enter the US with $100 worth of gifts from abroad. There are restrictions on bringing fresh fruit and flowers into the country and a strict quarantine on animals. Should you be carrying more than $10,000 in US or foreign cash, traveler's checks or money orders, you need to declare the excess amount.

Duty Free

US Customs allows each person over the age of 21 to bring 1L of liquor and 200 cigarettes duty free into the USA.

Departure Tax

An airport departure tax of $24 is charged to passengers traveling between the USA and foreign cities. If you purchase your ticket in the USA, the tax will normally be included in the price. Tickets purchased abroad may not include this tax. Visitors arriving from a foreign country will be charged a $6.50 North American Free Trade Agreement (Nafta) tax, which also may be included in the price of your ticket. To pay for added airport security since September 11, 2001, the US government has imposed a $2.50 tax per flight.

GETTING AROUND

The compact French Quarter is easily explored on foot. The St Charles streetcar is scenic and handy. Public buses connect major corridors, and most routes eventually feed into Canal St. Bikes are also an option thanks to the flat terrain.

Travel Passes

RTA (Regional Transit Authority; ☎ 248-3900; e www.norta.com) operates the public buses and streetcars. An all-day pass is $5 and available when boarding, from area hotels or from the RTA office (4th fl, 101 Dauphine St; 6, H3). A three-day pass is $12.

Bus

Buses are viable options for daytime travel to Mid-City (Nos 41, 42, 43), City Park (No 48 Esplanade), Faubourg Marigny and Bywater (No 5 Marigny/Bywater) and uptown along Magazine St (No 11 Magazine). Traveling at night to points unknown is not recommended as this increases your risk of theft. One-way travel is $1.25 (exact change only), and route maps can be obtained from the tourist office at 529 St Ann St (6, G6). Be warned that routes change at random.

Streetcar

There are two working streetcar lines; with a third (running the length of Canal St) scheduled to begin in mid-2004. The St Charles streetcar does a 13.5 mile loop from Canal and Carondelet Sts uptown along St Charles Ave. At the bend in the river, the streetcar turns onto S Carrollton St. Streetcars usually run every 20mins during peak times and less frequently during off-peak, 24hrs a day.

The wheelchair-accessible Riverfront line travels 2 miles from the Old US Mint to the Convention Center, with the French Market and Aquarium of the Americas as stops in between. The Riverfront line is $1.50.

Taxi

If traveling at night or alone, taxis are highly recommended. United Cab (☎ 522-9771) has reliable, courteous drivers. Telephone calls for a pickup are usually answered promptly, but prescheduled pickups are subject to error. Fares from the French Quarter to the Bywater are around $8, to the Garden District $10 or more, and to Mid-City $10; add an additional $1 for more than one passenger and a 15% tip. During Jazz Fest, there is a $3 special events fare from the French Quarter to the Fair Grounds, but availability is limited.

Bicycle

Bicycle rentals are available through French Quarter Bicycles (522 Dumaine St; 6, G6; ☎ 529-3136) and nearby in the Faubourg Marigny from Bicycle Michael's (622 Frenchmen St; 6, E8; ☎ 945-9505) for $15-20/day.

Adhere to one-way street rules to avoid hassles with aggressive drivers. Royal St will take you from the French Quarter into the CBD (where it turns into St Charles Ave once you cross Canal St) and uptown to Audubon Park. Burgundy St pierces into the Faubourg Marigny and Bywater. Esplanade Ave is a lovely ride to City Park. Magazine St can be a little tense with traffic.

One drawback is that drivers don't like to share the road with bikes. When it is safe, allow them enough room to pass. Also take care in locking your bike and all detachable parts before leaving it unattended. If someone asks you for the time, keep riding, as this is usually the prelude to a holdup.

Car & Motorcycle

The residents of New Orleans are incorrigibly dependent on the automobile and uncharacteristically aggressive when behind the wheel. For visitors, however, cars are convenient only if off-street parking is guaranteed and extensive travel outside the city is required. Most hotels have parking garages and charge $16-25/day. Parking meters offer 12mins for a quarter with a 2hr limit. Don't push your luck as the meter attendants are notoriously ruthless and will even issue tickets to 'just married' cars. The U-Park Garage (716 Iberville St; 6, J4; ☎ 522-5975), near the upper end of Bourbon St, charges $5 for the first hour or $19 for 24hrs. Other garages concentrated in the upper area of the Quarter charge similar rates.

If you park your car in a driveway, within 20ft of a corner or crosswalk, within 15ft of a fire hydrant or on a street-sweeping day, you will need about $75 (cash or credit card) plus cab fare (do not walk) to retrieve your car from the Auto Pound (400 N Claiborne Ave; 6, F2; ☎ 565-7450).

Road Rules

Drive on the right-hand side of the road. In town, speed limits range from 15mph in school zones to 40mph; highways kick it up from 55mph to 65mph. Wearing safety belts is required by law.

Rental

Rates for car rentals are $25-30/day, with hikes and limited availability at weekends. Because of a complicated mess of taxes, it is cheaper to rent from downtown New Orleans than the airport. Some companies allow you to return the vehicle to the airport without an extra charge; ask when making reservations.

Avis 2024 Canal St (☎ 523-4317, 800-3311-1212)

Budget 1317 Canal St (6, H2; ☎ 565-5600, 800-527-0700)

Enterprise 1939 Canal St (☎ 522-7900, 800-325-8007)

Hertz 901 Convention Center Blvd (5, H9; ☎ 568-1645, 800-654-3131)

Driving License & Permit

Visitors can drive in the US with a license from their home country and an international driving permit for up to 12 months.

Motoring Organizations

AAA (☎ 800-874-7532; e www.aaa .com) membership entitles you to 24hr roadside assistance as well as discounts at car-rental agencies and hotels.

PRACTICAL INFORMATION

Climate & When to Go

From February to April, New Orleans' subtropical climate is at its most agreeable (64-84°F or 18-29°C), coinciding with the city's best festivals (Mardi Gras and Jazz Fest).

This is also when rates are at their highest. Summer is unfathomably hot and humid with temperatures often above 100°F (38°C); for an added dose of fun, June to October is hurricane season. Summer, however, is an inexpensive and less crowded time to visit. September and October cool down to pleasant. Christmas is an off-peak period, and the weather is unseasonably warm (45°-64°F or 8-18°C) compared to that of northern locales. Hotel rates soar for the New Year's Eve Sugar Bowl football game.

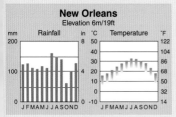

New Orleans
Elevation 6m/19ft

Tourist Information

Tourist Information Abroad

The USA does not have a well-developed system of overseas tourist offices. Contact your local US diplomatic office to obtain information from the United States Travel & Tourism Administration (USTTA).

France
  Claude Teboul of France Louisiane de la Nouvelle Orléans
  28 Blvd de Strasbourg, 75010 Paris (☎ 01 45 77 09 68)

UK
  New Orleans & Louisiana Tourist Office
  (☎ 020-8760-0377); no walk-in facilities

Local Tourist Information

The welcome center offers maps, pocket guidebooks, listings of upcoming events, a variety of brochures and discount RTA passes.

The visitors bureau distributes material on New Orleans culture, including a free visitor guide geared toward African Americans, *The Soul of New Orleans*.

New Orleans Welcome Center
  529 St Ann St (6, G6; ☎ 566-5031)

Metropolitan Convention & Visitors Bureau
  1520 Sugar Bowl Dr, New Orleans, LA 70112 (5, D3; ☎ 566-5011; e www.neworleanscvb.com)

NPS Visitor Center
  419 Decatur St (6, H5; ☎ 589-2636)

Louisiana Office of Tourism
  PO Box 94291, Baton Rouge, LA 70804 (☎ 342-8119, 800-414-8626)

Consulates

Check the Yellow Pages phone book under 'Consulates' for diplomatic representation. Canada does not have a consulate in New Orleans; the nearest is in Miami.

France
  1340 Poydras St (5, D4; ☎ 523-5772)

Japan
  639 Loyola Ave (5, E4; ☎ 529-2101)

Mexico
  2 Canal St (5, E9; ☎ 522-3596)

Spain
  2 Canal St (5, E9; ☎ 525-4951)

Switzerland
  1620 8th St (3, F11; ☎ 897-6510)

UK
  321 St Charles Ave (5, D7; ☎ 524-4180)

Money

Currency

The mighty US dollar is divided into 100 cents (¢) with coins of 1¢ (penny), 5¢ (nickel), 10¢ (dime), 25¢ (quarter) and the relatively rare 50¢ (half dollar). Quarters are the most commonly used coins in vending machines and parking meters, so it's handy to have a stash of them. Bills come in denominations of $1, $2, $5, $10, $20, $50 and $100.

Traveler's Checks

Traveler's checks are virtually as good as cash in the USA; you do not have to go to a bank to cash a traveler's check, as most establishments accept the checks just like cash. The major advantage of traveler's checks over cash is that they can be replaced if lost or stolen.

Credit Cards

Major credit cards are widely accepted. The most commonly accepted cards are Visa, MasterCard and American Express. However, Discover and Diners Club cards are also accepted by a fair number of businesses.

American Express	☎ 800-528-4800
Diners Club	☎ 800-234-6377
MasterCard	☎ 800-826-2181
Visa	☎ 800-336-8472

ATMs

You can easily obtain cash from ATMs all over New Orleans with a debit or credit card on the Plus or Cirrus system. The advantage of using ATMs is that you do not need to buy traveler's checks in advance, you do not have to pay the usual 1% commission on the checks, and if you're from a foreign country, you receive a better exchange rate. Area banks include Hibernia, Bank One and Whitney.

To avoid the withdrawal fee, which is $2-2.50 plus your home bank charge, go into the bank and ask a teller to perform a cash withdrawal; this circumvents all fees but is not as convenient as an ATM.

Changing Money

At the airport, Travelex (☎ 465-9647) and Whitney National Bank (☎ 838-6492) change money and are only a few feet apart for easy comparison. Better exchange rates are generally available in the CBD at the Hibernia National Bank (313 Carondelet St; 5, D6; ☎ 533-5712)

and Whitney National Bank's main office (228 St Charles Ave; 5, D7; ☎ 586-7272).

Banks are generally open Mon-Thurs 10am-5pm, Fri 10am-6pm and Sat 10am-1pm.

Tipping

Tipping is not really optional in the USA. In bars and restaurants, the waitstaff are paid minimal wages and rely upon tips for their livelihoods. Tip at least 15% of the bill or 20% if the service is great. You needn't tip at fast-food restaurants or self-serve cafeterias. Leave a dollar in the tip jar every time you buy a drink at a bar.

Taxi drivers expect a 15% tip. If you stay at a top-end hotel, tip the hotel porters $1 per bag, or more if you're importing bowling balls; smaller services (holding the taxi door open for you) might justify only $1. Leave $2 behind for the housecleaning staff. Valet parking is worth about $2, to be given when your car is returned to you.

Discounts

Admission to museums and area attractions is usually discounted for children, seniors and students. Visit e www.neworleansdiscounts.com for coupons to area attractions.

Student & Youth Cards

Present your student ID for discounts. As long as the little ones don't look like Britney Spears, most places will accept the age that parents report for their children without proof.

Seniors' Cards

Significant discounts are available with membership of the American Association of Retired Persons (AARP; 601 E St NW, Washington, DC 20049; ☎ 202-434-2277), representing Americans aged 50 years or older.

Travel Insurance

A policy covering theft, loss, medical expenses and compensation for cancellation or delays in your travel arrangements is highly recommended. If items are lost or stolen, make sure you get a police report straight away – otherwise your insurer might not pay up.

Opening Hours

Official business hours are Mon-Fri 9am-5pm, with abbreviated schedules on Saturday and closures on Sunday. But time is in the eye of the beholder in the Big Easy. The French Quarter tends to keep more reliable hours and weekend openings than elsewhere in the city.

Public Holidays

1 Jan	New Year's Day
3rd Mon in Jan	Martin Luther King Jr Day
3rd Mon in Feb	Presidents' Day
Feb/Mar	Mardi Gras Day
Mar/Apr	Easter Sunday
last Mon in May	Memorial Day
4 Jul	Independence Day
1st Mon in Sept	Labor Day
2nd Mon in Oct	Columbus Day
11 Nov	Veteran's Day
25 Dec	Christmas Day

Time

The USA uses the 12hr clock. Standard Time is 6hrs behind GMT/UTC. Daylight-savings time is practiced from the 1st Sunday of April, when clocks are advanced 1hr, to the last Saturday of October, when they retreat 1hr.

At noon in New Orleans it's:

1pm in New York
10am in Los Angeles
6pm in London
8pm in Johannesburg
7am (following day) in Auckland
5am (following day) in Sydney

Electricity

Electric current in the USA is 110-115V, 60Hz AC. Outlets are suited to flat two-prong or three-prong grounded plugs. If your appliance is made for another electrical system, you will need a transformer or adapter or both.

Weights & Measures

The USA stubbornly holds on to the imperial system, unfazed that the rest of the world uses the metric system. Gasoline is measured in the US gallon. Temperatures are in degrees Fahrenheit, whereby 32°F is freezing. See the conversion table on p. 122.

Post

The main New Orleans post office (701 Loyola Ave; 5, F4; ☎ 589-1706) is near City Hall. Smaller branches can be found in the Airport Mail Center (in the passenger terminal; 1, C9); the World Trade Center (2 Canal St; 5, E9; ☎ 523-6127); the Vieux Carré (1022 Iberville St; 6, H3; ☎ 525-4896); and the CBD at Lafayette Square (610 S Maestri Place; 5, F7; ☎ 581-1039).

In the French Quarter, there are independent postal shops, including Royal Mail Service (828 Royal St; 6, G6; ☎ 522-8523) and the French Quarter Postal Emporium (1000 Bourbon St; 6, F6; ☎ 525-6651). These shops will send letters and packages at the same rates as the post office.

Postal Rates

Postal rates frequently increase, but at the time of writing, the rates were 37¢ for 1st-class mail within the USA for letters up to 1oz (23¢ for each additional ounce) and 23¢ for postcards.

International airmail to places other than Canada and Mexico is 80¢ for a 1oz letter and 70¢ for a postcard. It costs 60¢ to send a 1oz letter and 50¢ to send a postcard to Canada and Mexico. Aerogrammes are 70¢.

Opening Hours
Post offices are generally open Mon-Fri 8:30am-4:30pm and Sat 8:30am-noon.

Telephone
Local calls from a pay phone generally cost 35¢.

Phonecards
Phone debit cards are readily available and sold at newsstands and pharmacies. Lonely Planet's ekno Communication Card, specifically aimed at travellers, provides competitive rates on international calls (avoid using it for local calls), messaging services and free email. Log on to **e** www.ekno.lonelyplanet.com for more information.

Mobile Phones
The USA uses a variety of mobile phone systems, only one of which is remotely compatible with systems used outside North America. Check with your provider to determine coverage and avoid roaming charges.

Country & City Codes
USA	☎ 1
New Orleans	☎ 504

Useful Numbers
Local Directory Inquiries	☎ 411
International Directory Inquiries	☎ 412-555-1515
Reverse-Charge (Collect)	☎ 0
Time	☎ 529-6111
Weather/Hurricane	☎ 800-672-6124

International Direct Dial Codes
Dial ☎ 011 followed by:
Australia	☎ 61
Japan	☎ 81
New Zealand	☎ 64
South Africa	☎ 27
UK	☎ 44

Electronic Resources
Free Internet usage is available at the public library (219 Loyola Ave; 5, C5; ☎ 529-7323), near City Hall, but waiting times can exceed an hour.

Internet Service Providers
Check with your home ISP for access numbers so that you can dial-up the Internet from New Orleans. If you're a client of Earthlink dial ☎ 654-0020; for AOL dial ☎ 620-0800.

Internet Cafés
If you can't access the Internet from where you're staying, head to a cybercafe:

Bastille Computer Café
  605 Toulouse St (6, H5; ☎ 581-1150; open 10am-11pm; $2.75/15mins, $4.75/30mins)

Contemporary Arts Center
  900 Camp St (5, G6; ☎ 523-0990; open 11am-5pm; free 30mins usage with café purchase)

Royal Access
  621 Royal St (6, G5; ☎ 525-0401; open Mon-Fri 9am-8pm, Sat-Sun 9am-10pm; $3/15mins, $5/30mins)

Useful Sites
The Lonely Planet website (**e** www.lonelyplanet.com) offers a speedy link to many of New Orleans' websites. Others to try include:

New Orleans Online
  e www.neworleansonline.com

Times-Picayune
  e www.nolalive.com

Offbeat Magazine
  e www.offbeat.com

WWOZ Radio (great links)
e www.wwoz.org

Save Our Cemeteries
e www.saveourcemeteries.org

Mardi Gras Indians
e www.mardigrasindians.com

Louisiana Music Factory
e www.louisianamusicfactory.com

Jazz Festival
e www.insideneworleans.com/hp/content
/events/music/jazzfest/

CitySync

CitySync New Orleans, Lonely Planet's digital guide for Palm OS hand-held devices, allows quick searches, sorting and bookmarking of hundreds of New Orleans' attractions, clubs, hotels, restaurants and more – all pinpointed on scrollable street maps. Purchase or demo CitySync New Orleans at e www .citysync.com.

Doing Business

Most hotels in the CBD offer comprehensive business centers. Temporary office space in the business district is available through Kensington Business Centres (☎ 877-725-1762). Alpha Tech Communications (4440 Chastant St, Metairie; ☎ 454-6554) provides interpreting and translation services.

New Orleans is a popular destination for conventions and large-scale meetings. The Ernest N Morial Convention Center (900 Convention Center Blvd; 5, H10; ☎ 582-3023; e www.mccno.com) has 140 meeting rooms, exhibition space and a convenient location. The New Orleans Metropolitan Convention & Visitors Bureau (☎ 566-5011; e www.neworleanscvb.com) can assist with meeting planning. The mayor's office runs a department of international relations and trade development (☎ 565-7230).

Newspapers & Magazines

New Orleans' only daily newspaper, the *Times-Picayune*, costs 50¢ Mon-Sat and $1.50 Sunday. Don't miss the Friday 'Lagniappe' entertainment guide. The *Times-Picayune* is perhaps the only US newspaper that includes occasional editorials on French issues.

Louisiana Weekly, published in New Orleans since 1925, offers an African-American perspective on local and regional politics and events.

For entertainment listings, pick up a copy of the free weekly newspaper *Gambit*. The free monthly *Offbeat* magazine provides a complete music and entertainment calendar with good reviews of local performances

Radio

Listener-supported WWOZ-FM 90.7 offers jazz, with a mix of blues, R&B and Cajun. The DJs keep you posted on all the comings and goings of the city's homegrown talent.

Station WWNO-FM 89.9 is the city's only National Public Radio affiliate, offering morning and evening news programs.

The newscasters on WRBH-FM 88.3 read the local paper on air for the blind and print-handicapped.

A zydeco music show is hosted by Kateri Yager every Saturday 10am-1pm on WSLA 1560 AM.

TV

The local PBS affiliate WYES Channel 12 runs educational programming and documentaries on Acadian culture and wetland ecology. WWLChannel 4 features a 2hr cooking show with local celebrity Frank Davis.

Photography & Video

Liberty Camera Center (337 Caron-delet St; 5, D6; ☎ 523-6252) and Downtown Fast Foto (327 St Charles Ave; 5, D7; ☎ 525-2598) offer quick color print and E-6 slide processing.

Overseas visitors shopping for videos must remember that the US uses the NTSC system, which is incompatible with the PAL (UK and Australasia) and SECAM (Western Europe) formats.

Health

Immunizations

For most foreign visitors no immun-izations are required for entry, though cholera and yellow fever vaccinations may be required of travelers from areas with a history of those diseases.

Precautions

Tap water is drinkable if not particu-larly delicious. Be sure to drink lots of water to avoid dehydration, especially when the days are hot. Wear sunscreen and a hat and walk in the shade to avoid heat exhaus-tion and sunburn.

Insurance & Medical Treatment

Travel insurance is advisable to cover any medical treatment you may need while in New Orleans. Medical attention in the US is expensive, and many drugs available over the counter in foreign countries require a prescription in the US.

Medical Services

Hospitals with 24hr accident and emergency departments include the Medical Center of Louisiana (also called Charity Hospital) at 1532 Tulane Ave (5, B4; ☎ 903-2311).

Dental Services

If you chip a tooth or require emer-gency treatment, contact the New Orleans Dental Association (☎ 834-6449), which can refer you to an ADA-affiliated dentist within your insurance group or at least nearby.

Pharmacies

The following pharmacies are open 24hrs or have long opening hours. Walgreens (☎ 800-289-2273) has several locations within walking distance of the French Quarter. A 24hr Rite Aid (3, F11; ☎ 896-4575) can be found at 3401 St Charles Ave at Louisiana Ave.

Toilets

Public toilets are a rare breed in the Quarter. Two have been spotted at Jackson Brewery mall (6, H6; 620 Decatur St) and French Market (6, F7). But lots of restaurants and bars are happy to have you as a patron, even if the obligatory drink is only an excuse.

Safety Concerns

New Orleans' beguiling quaintness tricks tourists into thinking they are in a small village rather than a large, economically depressed city. There is a razor's edge of danger here, which requires big city alertness. New Orleans is a checkerboard of poor and rich areas, where the mansions of the Garden District can quickly give way to boarded up buildings and 'locals' only' neighborhoods. By day you are more likely to be in well-traveled areas where muggings and other violence are less likely. If you notice you're the only one around and your instincts start to itch, heed them. Areas you should avoid on foot include the Tremé district (on the lake side of Rampart St), the Irish Channel neighborhood (on the river side of Magazine St) and deep sec-tions of the Bywater. At night you should take a cab or drive to bars, restaurants and nightclubs outside of the Quarter.

Lost Property

Call RTA's office (☎ 248-3900) to report lost items.

Keeping Copies

Make photocopies of all your important documents, keep some with you, separate from the originals, and leave a copy at home. You can also store details of documents in Lonely Planet's free online Travel Vault, password-protected and accessible worldwide. See e www .ekno.lonelyplanet.com.

Emergency Numbers

Ambulance	☎ 911
Fire	☎ 911
Police (emergency)	☎ 911
Police (non-emergency)	☎ 821-2222
Rape Crisis Line	☎ 483-8888

Women Travelers

Women will feel perfectly safe traveling around solo by day in New Orleans. But in bars and clubs, the city's natural friendliness can quickly erode into unwanted advances. Use Southern manners to deflect the liquid-courage crowd (if that fails, give a gracious smile as you move to the other end of the bar).

Tampons and over-the-counter contraceptives are widely available. Birth control pills are available by prescription only. Planned Parenthood (☎ 897-9200; 4018 Magazine St) provides health care services for women, including pregnancy testing and birth control counseling.

Gay & Lesbian Travelers

The gay community has a firm grip on the outer Quarter, where many businesses are gay-owned and operated. Lesbians keep a much lower profile in the Faubourg Marigny and the Bywater. Finding a place to stay, eat or party for gay visitors in New Orleans will be a question of individual tastes not fear of discrimination.

Information & Organizations

Visit the Lesbian & Gay Community Center (2114 Decatur St; 6, F8; ☎ 945-1103) to get a better dish on the local landscape. Faubourg Marigny Book Store (600 Frenchman St; 6, E8; ☎ 943-9875) is the South's oldest gay bookstore. The *Weekly Guide* is a free pamphlet chock-full of information about gay and lesbian businesses, entertainment venues, hotels and guesthouses. Other rags on the scene include *Southern Voice*, *Ambush Magazine* and the *Whiz Magazine*.

Senior Travelers

New Orleans is a great place for seniors, who are usually the last ones standing after the younger hotshots have stumbled off to bed. Elderhostel (☎ 877-426-8056; e www.elderhostel.org) offers weeklong educational tours of New Orleans and the surrounding area.

Disabled Travelers

All federally funded institutions are handicapped-accessible thanks to US law. But historic houses are exempt from this and do not have elevators or ramps. Hotels are obligated to provide wheelchair access, although accessible bathrooms are primarily found at newer properties. Wheelchair ramps and/or elevators are available at the ferry crossings. For information about paratransit service, call the RTA (☎ 827-7433). The Riverfront streetcar line features braille kiosks, platform ramps and wide doors that allow anyone to board easily. Unfortunately, the St Charles streetcar line has not been modified for wheelchair passengers.

The French Quarter is especially difficult for disabled travelers. Beware the rough masonry of sidewalks that hinder wheelchair travel.

Information & Organizations

American Red Cross (☎ 586-8191), Catholic Deaf Center (☎ 486-6345) and Lighthouse for the Blind (☎ 899-4501) can provide specialized advice and services for disabled individuals.

Language

New Orleanians speak English, kind of. French heritage has left a lot of foreign terms in the local lexicon as well as imparted a Gallic spin on pronunciation. The New Orleans accent is unique, at times sounding more like a Brooklyn day laborer than a Deep South belle. It reflects the influences of the Irish, Italian and German immigrants of the turn of the 20th century. The heaviest of these accents are sometimes lovingly and despairingly referred to as 'y'ats' because of the common greeting 'Where y'at.'

andouille (ahn-**doo**-we) – the Creole version of this French sausage is ground pork in casings made from smoked pig intestines

banquette – a diminutive form of 'banc,' meaning bench, applied to the early wooden boardwalks; it's sometimes used today to refer to sidewalks

bayou – a natural canal of sluggish and marshy water removed from the main river channel

beignet (ben-**yea**) - a deep-fried pastry that is New Orleans' version of the doughnut; it's typically covered with powdered sugar

boudin – a Cajun sausage filled with pork, pork liver and rice

café au lait – a mixture of coffee and steamed milk; Creole coffee is a blend of roasted coffee beans (60%) and chicory root (40%)

Cajun – Louisianans descended from French-speaking Acadia; the term may also apply to other rural settlers who live amid Cajuns; a corruption of Acadian

Creole – a free person of French, Spanish or African descent born in Spanish America

dirty rice – small quantities of giblets or ground pork, along with green onions, peppers and celery, fried with rice

etouffee (ay-too-**fay**) – a spicy tomato-based stew that typically includes crawfish, shrimp or chicken and is served with rice

gallery – a balcony or roofed promenade

go-cup – a plastic container provided so patrons can leave a bar with a drink; it's legal to drink alcoholic beverages in the street, but it's illegal to carry an open glass container

gris-gris – magical objects said to have curative, protective or evil powers; used in voodoo

gumbo – traditionally an African soup thickened with okra, containing seafood or chicken; Cajun gumbos substitute a filé powder for okra

krewe – a variation of 'crew,' meaning a club (usually with an exclusive membership) that sponsors Mardi Gras parades and other events

jambalaya – leftovers go into this one-dish meal of rice cooked with ham, onions, peppers and celery

lagniappe – a small gift from a merchant or resident; literally, it's a little something extra

meuniere (muhn-**yair**) – seasoned fish, coated lightly with flour and pan-fried in butter; it's served with a lemon-butter sauce

neutral ground – the Canal St median that served as a neutral meeting space dividing the Creole and American communities

red beans and rice – a spicy bean stew with peppers, many seasonings and a hunk of salt pork, served over white rice

rémoulade (reh-moo-**laud**) – a sauce with a mayonnaise base and a variety of ingredients such as pickles, herbs, capers and mustard; crawfish or shrimp rémoulade is often a cold noodle salad

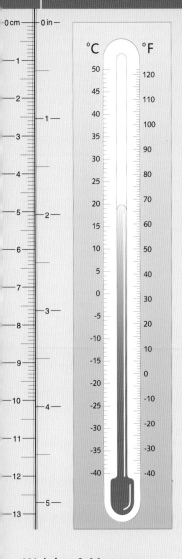

Conversion Table

Clothing Sizes
Measurements approximate only; try before you buy.

Women's Clothing

Aust/NZ	8	10	12	14	16	18
Europe	36	38	40	42	44	46
Japan	5	7	9	11	13	15
UK	8	10	12	14	16	18
USA	6	8	10	12	14	16

Women's Shoes

Aust/NZ	5	6	7	8	9	10
Europe	35	36	37	38	39	40
France only	35	36	38	39	40	42
Japan	22	23	24	25	26	27
UK	3½	4½	5½	6½	7½	8½
USA	5	6	7	8	9	10

Men's Clothing

Aust/NZ	92	96	100	104	108	112
Europe	46	48	50	52	54	56
Japan	S		M	M		L
UK	35	36	37	38	39	40
USA	35	36	37	38	39	40

Men's Shirts (Collar Sizes)

Aust/NZ	38	39	40	41	42	43
Europe	38	39	40	41	42	43
Japan	38	39	40	41	42	43
UK	15	15½	16	16½	17	17½
USA	15	15½	16	16½	17	17½

Men's Shoes

Aust/NZ	7	8	9	10	11	12
Europe	41	42	43	44½	46	47
Japan	26	27	27.5	28	29	30
UK	7	8	9	10	11	12
USA	7½	8½	9½	10½	11½	12½

Weights & Measures

Weight

1kg = 2.2lb
1lb = 0.45kg
1g = 0.04oz
1oz = 28g

Volume

1 liter = 0.26 US gallons
1 US gallon = 3.8 liters
1 liter = 0.22 imperial gallons
1 imperial gallon = 4.55 liters

Length & Distance

1 inch = 2.54cm
1cm = 0.39 inches
1m = 3.3ft = 1.1yds
1ft = 0.3m
1km = 0.62 miles
1 mile = 1.6km

lonely planet

Lonely Planet is the world's most successful independent travel information company with offices in Australia, the USA, UK and France. With a reputation for comprehensive, reliable travel information, Lonely Planet is a print and electronic publishing leader, with over 650 titles and 22 series catering for travelers' individual needs.

At Lonely Planet we believe that travelers can make a positive contribution to the countries they visit – if they respect their host communities and spend their money wisely. Since 1986 a percentage of the income from books has been donated to aid and human rights projects.

www.lonelyplanet.com

For news, views and free subscriptions to print and email newsletters, and a full list of LP titles, click on Lonely Planet's award-winning website.

On the Town

A romantic escape to Paris or a mad shopping dash through New York City, the locals' secret bars or a city's top attractions – whether you have 24hrs to kill or months to explore, Lonely Planet's On the Town products will give you the low-down.

Condensed guides are ideal pocket guides for when time is tight. Their quick-view maps, full-colour layout and opinionated reviews help short-term visitors target the top sights and discover the very best eating, shopping and entertainment options a city has to offer.

For more indepth coverage, **City guides** offer insights into a city's character and cultural background as well as providing extensive coverage of where to eat, stay and play. **CitySync**, a digital guide for your handheld unit, allows you to reference stacks of opinionated, well-researched travel information. Portable and durable **City Maps** are perfect for locating those back-street bars or hard-to-find local haunts.

'Ideal for a generation of fast movers.'

– *Gourmet Traveller* on Condensed guides

Condensed Guides

- Amsterdam
- Athens
- Bangkok
- Barcelona
- Beijing (Sept 2003)
- Boston
- Brussels (March 2004)
- Chicago
- Dublin
- Florence (May 2003)
- Frankfurt
- Hong Kong
- Las Vegas (May 2003)
- Lisbon (March 2004)
- London
- Los Angeles
- Madrid
- Milan (March 2004)
- New Orleans
- New York City
- Paris
- Prague
- Rome
- San Francisco
- Singapore
- Sydney
- Tokyo
- Venice
- Washington, DC

index

See also separate indexes for Places to Eat (p. 126), Places to Stay (p. 127), Shops (p. 127) and Sights with map references (p. 128).

PLACES TO EAT

PLACES TO STAY

SHOPS

sights – quick index